REFLECTIONS
"Memories of a Life"

Sidney Kaplan
Baltimore, Maryland

REFLECTIONS   "Memories of a Life"

by Sidney Kaplan

First Edition - January, 2000

Orders:
Forty-One West Partnership
11 East Mount Royal Avenue
Baltimore, Maryland 21202
(410) 752-2090 Phone
(410) 783-2723 Fax

ISBN 0-9678505-0-9

Printed in the United States of America

TABLE OF CONTENTS

My Book

It may not a best-seller be,

But much of this is part of me,

Prior lives for my children to see.

4/9/89

Φ Φ Φ

Prologue

Why Write Poetry?
Who or What Motivated Me?
When Did I Start?

The truth is that I do not remember who motivated me to start writing verse. I do not remember when it started. My first recollection of writing poetry came when I was 10 years old. The first poem I remember writing was about the French and Indian Wars when I was a student in grade school. It was 1932, the year my father died. I do not have a copy of that poem.

The same year I wrote of my experiences at the Sydenham Hospital. The poem is titled "I Went to the Hospital" and it was written while in the hospital. Someone, perhaps my mother, must have suggested that I show the poem to the newspaper. In those years each paper had weekly sections devoted to poetry.

I recall taking a copy of the poem to the Baltimore News Post. I recall the large room with a series of desks and my being led to the desk of a reporter. He listened to my story, had my picture taken and agreed to publish the poem. Behold, I was published!

I continued writing verse.

Throughout my years, I have found it relaxing to pen my

thoughts in verse. It was, and is, a continuing challenge to look around me, see life, and pen the things I see; the thoughts I have; my innermost desires and my dreams.

Serving in the United States Marine Corps in WWII, I continued to write verse relaying my experiences and again my thoughts. During these years of extensive letter writing I also wrote prose, my journals. I could not let my letters be stereotyped. A few lines of verse were best able to express my innermost desires and my dreams.

In later years I would gain a thought, write a few lines of verse, and place them in a folder to form the basis for some future poem.

Writing poetry became contagious. My grandchildren, without exception, began to write poetry. Some of what they wrote jolted me with its depth and maturity.

I wrote for them - they wrote for me.

My earliest recollection of a poem came several years before my father died. I would regularly spend the night at my maternal grandmother's house. When I did, I often went to the Enoch Pratt Library. I recall one such visit. I recall the substance of the poem I read. (I do not remember there being any books in my home or my grandmother's home.)

The poem was about turtles. It was the story of a male turtle who lost his mate. It told of the close relationship the turtle had with his mate. What I most remember is that when the female turtle died, the male had to immediately seek another mate. At this age, 7 or 8 years, the moral made an indelible impression on me. I cannot understand why so mature a subject would dig so deeply into my child's mind, but it did.

Throughout my mature years I have witnessed the truth of the story. Time after time I have seen aged partners, both friends and family, who had lived devotedly with each other, respond in like fashion when a partner died. The one who survived had to have another mate. The poem of the turtle became even more indelible.

I do not remember a single line of the turtle poem. I do not remember the name of the poem. I do not remember the name of the author. I do, however, remember the story.

Is that not evidence of the indelible nature of verse? It's neither the rhyme nor rhythm that matters; it's the life experiences that poetry relates that are everlasting. It's poetry's capacity to interpret the acts of man and the mystic powers of nature.

Format

The contents of this collection are divided into categories and placed accordingly. Let it be understood that no matter how thorough I tried to be, I found that in many writings the categories are not sharply divisive. The same writing is often capable of belonging to more than one category; I have, however, called the category I thought most acceptable.

All the writings are dated where dates are known. My mistake has been not to have dated my 'first thoughts' notes, so that when I later attempted to finalize the writing I was in a dilemma. Should I use the 'first thoughts' dates (if available) or should I use the refinement dates?

In many instances because of personal preference I have added an explanatory note preceding the writings. The prime purpose of these notes is to allow my children to know what prompted the 'first thoughts' and what my status in life was at that time.

LOVE

Only Honor

"Only Honor", he replied,
"Only Honor, nothing more,"
*"Only Hono*r" and she sighed,
*"Only Hono*r, nothing more."

How she loved him no words could say;
Each night retired, the way she'd pray
That they together would find a way.

But, Only Honor, those words rang true.
Only Honor, what could they do?

*"It just was not meant to be,
God did not mean him for me".*

*"When he is near my senses shudder,
The thought that he belongs to another.
My heart is torn, my brain I rack;
But I dare not call him back.*

*"And so I turn and try to bear,
the knowing that he is not there.*

"And all the while I try to smile
To hide the pain within;
So real it seems, I can't stop dreams
Of how it might have been.

"Now there is nought else to do,
Better that my days were through."

And with the dark that came that night,
There was a spark and a ghastly sight--
One hand she held aside her breast,
And softly set her down to rest.

Then birds began to sing--
The pain she felt no more.
Gone was the bitter sting--
Her heart no longer sore.

May, 1942

Φ Φ Φ

Reliving

I would love to go thru time again

Reliving days I knew,

But only if in reliving them

The path would lead to you.

10/87

Φ Φ Φ

Need

When I most need you, I've come to know
Is when I have nowhere else to go.

When life fades and in despair I mourn
When hope seems lost and my heart is torn.

Then I most need you, your touch, your tears,
Two together, allaying all lifes fears.

Φ Φ Φ

Security Blanket

How can it be? As everyone can see
That to my own precious "honey Bea"

I have become a covering cloth.
The ingredients of chicken broth.

However else am I to rank it?
I've become her security blanket.

Φ Φ Φ

Sharing

Together we have grown from a very humble start
Living thru life's moments, it's rarely that we part.
Knowing the secrets of the dictates of my heart
Saddened when my movements wander into wrought.

You're my better judgment, the good that lies within
Knowing right and do not waiver to my every whim.
You have made our home just what every home should be
It's a place of calmness among the roaring sea.

Learning that the secret of all life is living,
Learning that the secret of our love is giving.
First a wedding ring, then hearing children sing.
Sad and happy days, memories are everything.

And although there are many things that I have not done
So very many things that perhaps I may never do.
For I know that the best of all things I've done.
Is living and sharing my every day with you.

1/25/89
London

Φ Φ Φ

I Care

There was the beginning, so many
    years ago,
Tears and tribulations from which
    memories flow.
Trying days and better days with most
    of life's fare.
    Thru it all, always know
    "that I care."

Tender moments when we're alone.
Meeting life when all our deeds are shown.
Moments ne'er forgot, the dreams we share.
    Thru it all, always know
    "that I care."

The home which we have made
    together.
Travels that grow better and
    better.
Endless secrets of my lady's lair!
    Thru it all, always know
    "that I care."

Growing together, walking thru life's way.
Laughing together, times of work or play.
Times of plenty and when plates were bare.
    Thru it all, always know
    "that I care."

Creating life, miracles by
    you and me.
Now enthralled by the little
    lives we see.
Our watching each showing their own
    flim and flair..
    Thru it all, always know
    "that I care."

I know not what tomorrow
    will bring,
Or what type of songs our hearts
    will sing.
But whatever we do, or we dare,
    Thru it all, always know
    "that I care."

                 Sidney Kaplan
                 1/18/88

Φ Φ Φ

In my war letters, verse
Relaying emotions.

There By Me

Each night I close my eyes to dream,

And so real do my visions seem,

That I awaken, only to see,

If you are really there by me.

12/29/42

Φ Φ Φ

Absence

My God, I thank you for her love
    It's more than I am worthy of.
To hold, to kiss, to just caress
    Her love, her lips, her tenderness.
Please hear, my God, bring her to me.
    You alone know my agony.
With her away, I'd best not be.
    I pray to you for your mercy.

12/42

Φ Φ Φ

All is Love

My love with every word

My soul with every phrase

No truer Psalm is heard

Oh' God, I sing your praise.

2/12/43

Φ Φ Φ

Heavens Speak

Just when I felt the lips of life
And came to know my future wife,
Fate made it's move and destiny
Withheld my lady love from me.

My heart looked toward the sky
And saw the clouds go passing by
Then heard the heavens smile and say,
*"Be patient son await Your day.
Together you will see your sun
And hear many a little one."*

2/43

Φ Φ Φ

Depression

When dreary shades of doubt enclose

And darken out my mind

I seek a path from this repose

And you're the path I find.

4/25/43

Φ Φ Φ

Dreaming

Each night I wander far away

And rest beside you all the day.

And in my dreams I hear you say,

"I Love You."

Lt. Bea
6/24/43

Φ Φ Φ

Together

With the night I draw you near,
And hold your warmth so close,
And whisper that "I love you, dear,"
For it's you that I want most.

For now I dream of another era,
Where we both stand - man and wife,
Free of all this woe and care,
Free of all this fear and strife.

                                    Letter to Bea
                                    7/1/44

ΦΦΦ

Waiting-Anticipating

'Tis a beautiful day
'Tis a beautiful world
'Tis a beautiful maid whose
love my heart holds --

So little new to tell you --
Things are well --
My dreams full of only you --

Waiting -- sometimes with patience
    -- sometimes with desperation
Knowing the day is but a step ahead
Beginning to believe it will come
faster than I expected --

Prepare for the phone call --
Prepare for 'weak knees' --
POSSIBLY A DEEP THIRST

        Definitely me,

        Hawaii
        3rd October '45

Φ Φ Φ

To My Future Wife

MY THOUGHTS

What is life but that a man must live it---
The hidden abyss of the mind of a man so often untouched by
    the passing day; so often unknown to he who houses it---
Weariness, that time when the mind is lost and aware of its
    state---
How many men travel the span of days, from the day of birth
    to the day of death and from the beginning to the end of
    their travels know not life---
It is like the love for a woman---
Not love of body and not the complete absence of the love of
    body---
Not want of warmth for the sake of warmth---
Not want of companionship because of loneliness---
But love, the type of love that bears upon the person and upon
    all the person has shown herself to be---
A man and a woman--two apart when two are not meant to be
    apart---
Woman who blossoms only after she has known man---
And man---too often answering the urge as prompted but the
    urge alone---
Touching the purity of she who has been untouched---
And marring the virgin only for the sake of the moment.
Am I such a man?
Is this the love I hold?
Or is the feeling that rests in my heart born free of desire, yet
    full with dreams---
Dreams of a woman---

Not just any woman, but one who shares more than a
    common bed---one who shares the inner self, the mind
    that lives within as well as the body that lives without---
One who has come to know that where only presence can
    lend the touch of hand, that words and voice can lend
    comfort beyond that confine of space or time---
Or is all I say but words put forth for want of else to do---
Or is the madness of the moment beyond the understanding
    of the man who writes---
Loneliness can cause such pain---
Loneliness can twist the hours until the hours flood
    themselves with unraveled ramblings---
Confused state of affairs---
Unable to think---writing free of thought---
Having passed a third of life---a portion well weighed with
    trial and tear---
Having come so far and having found in her alone the
    essence of the years that have gone and the years that are
    yet to come---
Reaching the beauty for which a heart has cried---
Touching that beauty, not beauty of being nor beauty of the
    person but beauty of the truth of her love---
Coming so close and then torn away---
Knowing that days alone keep you from the full share of all
    two hearts hold to be shared---
Knowing this and longing all the more for the knowing---
Living in a world away from where you yourself reside---
Standing here and because of the strength of the love I hold
    not fully here---

Wanting you with every ounce of strength in my body---
Loving more than I dare admit---
Sometimes afraid of a love that controls the mind and is lost
     to the control of mind---
With a breath of reverence with the mention of her name---
Asking The Force that rests beyond us, to keep her mine, to
     make me worthy of her---
Knowing too well that if the time came when life had to be
     lived without her, the strength to live such a life would
     not be mine---
A fool's thoughts these are---
Free of censor--partially complete---
Telling you so little of all there is to tell---
In the beginning of the writing, the mood was one of
     restlessness and despondency---
     at the close, the mood although more calm, is much
     the same---
Only being with you for all the days of my life will make me
     what I am to be---
A man who in the earliest days of his youth has dreamed of a
     destiny that rests far beyond the scope of that thought
     he himself would dare discuss---
A man who knows that the future that is to come will come
     only because of a woman---
That without her the closing chapter will not read the same---

THAT SHE IS MORE THAN HIS HAPPINESS---
THAT SHE IS THE SOURCE OF STRENGTH WITHOUT
    WHICH TOMORROW COULD NOT BE---
THAT SHE IS ALL THIS NOT FOR WHAT SHE DOES
    BUT FOR WHAT SHE IS---
NOT BECAUSE OF WHAT SHE TRIES TO BE BUT FOR
    WHAT SHE IS FREE OF ALL EFFORT---
God alone knows the truths of tomorrow---
The tomorrow that will soon be with us.

                    Your 'husband', Sidney
                    10/9/46

      Φ Φ Φ

MOTHER

My Love for Mother

There is a spot in my heart,
That holds my love for mother,
It is a place, set well apart,
To be filled by no other.

With the passing of each year,
And the days that listfully go,
With each and every tender tear,
And each love I grow to know.

There will never come to be,
Nor has there ever been,
A love so dear to me,
As that love of closest kin.

Even though I've grown old,
And I've learned to love another,
There's that spot I'll ever hold,
The spot that belongs to Mother.

To Mother
1/7/43

Φ Φ Φ

A Mother's Love

Blessed are we for freedom and grace,
For the love in the smile on a mother's face,
For the dark of the night, and the dawn again,
For the privilege *'to live'* or *'to die'* FREE MEN.

Blessed indeed are all those mortal fools,
Whose crafts are carved with worldly tools,
But not for the things of material worth,
So much as *'that'* love given us at birth.

No man need walk the way of life,
And brood his mind, or live with strife,
For on this earth or in the heavens high above,
Each man is blessed with a mother's love.

And your son, just like all other men,
Knows best the meaning of that love when,
I need it most, as my eyes grow dim,
They brighten up, as I speak to Him.

For He has given to me, and to all,
The mightiest bond, a mother's call,
The voice that ever speaks forth to say,
"My son each night for you, I pray,
In solemn prayer I shed all fear,
And with the flow of a mother's tear,
I pray, you soon return, my dear."

To Mother -
February 1943

Φ Φ Φ

Name of Mother

The holiest words my tongue can frame,
The noblest thoughts my soul can claim,
Unworthy are to praise the name,
More sacred than all others.

An infant when her love first came,
A man I find it just the same,
Reverently I breathe the name,
The blessed name of mother.

4/27/45

Φ Φ Φ

Mother's Day

They say today is Mother's Day,

That it comes but once a year,

But everyday is Mother's Day,

Where I'm concerned, my dear.

5/1/43

Φ Φ Φ

Mom Mom

Some people send a Valentine

To say that "I Love You"

But we don't need a Valentine

Because you know we do.

Φ Φ Φ

CHILDREN

IMPRINTS

Thoughts of imprints on my mind,
The deepest prints of any kind,
Ageless prints that surpass time,
Memory of a nursery rhyme.

The many imprints made on me,
The thoughts that guide my destiny,
The patience of a dad at play,
The prayers I heard my mother pray.

And so to each I plead this truth
Imprints made on the mind of youth,
The way we sit, the things we teach,
The examples set, the words we preach.

Deep imprints that no matter what,
Are sown, and grow, and ne'er forgot
For as we sow, so shall we reap,
'Tis our life's way, our child will keep.

1/15/87

Φ Φ Φ

During World War II, I spent several years in the Marine Corps, my first experience being separated from my family and home.

Throughout my early life, I served as a substitute father to my brother and my sister. My brother was four years old and my sister was one year old when my father died.

While away from from home, my sister wrote to me saying that she was going to cut her hair short. Her jet-black silky hair fell well below her hips. I urged her to reconsider.

To Gloria

Behind her chubby cheeks of red
Fall two black pigtails from her head;
And of all your treasures, little maid,
Hold none so close as that flow of jade.

You can sail the waters far and wide,
You can scan the lands and the countryside;
And in all your search, where'ere you go,
You'll not find the likes of that silken flow.

Yours is a gift that few possess,
It ranks above all your loveliness,
Your soothing smile, your tender care,
The silken glow of your jet black hair.

Dear little sister, I plead with you,
Whatever else you may ever do,
Don't harm one strand, one single thread
Of that gorgeous growth upon your head.

6/3/43

Φ Φ Φ

My life has been many things, but none so endearing as being a father and a grandfather.

When my daughter was five-years old, her grandfather bought her a two-wheel bike. Her eyes sparkled when she saw the bike. She immediately decided that a bike was a thing to ride--and ride it she did!

The Bike

"Don't tell me what I cannot do!"
I told the doubting men.
"Don't tell me why I should not try
To reach the stars again!"

THE FIVE YEAR OLD
I saw her on that day so long ago
Her precious smile-lit face, her eyes aglow.

Taking bike in hand, to the grass she went
I'll not forget the way that day was spent!

There were only two wheels to this new bike
Unlike any prior one ridden by the tyke!

The fact that she had never ridden such
To her just did not seem to matter much.

I wondered if her bare baby feet
Would reach the pedals from the saddle seat?

She topped the bike and tried to ride,
Fell, skinned her knees but she never cried.

Each fall she got up and tried again.
Her little spirits refused to bend!

I watched both of her tiny knees bleed
Scratches on her legs, but she gave no heed.

Late that day, through all her pain and pride
I watched her on her bike. Ride, ride, ride!

She knew not what she could not do
  And so the task was done!
She knew not what she could not do
  And so her day she won!

Φ Φ Φ

Our Children Are

Our children are---
The best of we---
The worst of we---
Tranquilizers in a worried sea.

The freshness of a youthful face---
The warmth of a burning fireplace---
A source from which new
   life will sprout---
That's what this thing is all about.

1966
(Written in Italy)
"A Letter to my Little Girl"

Φ Φ Φ

On my daughter's wedding day I penned these thoughts.

Dream No Little Dreams

Dream no little dreams,
  Child of mine.
Seek life's wonders, and
  You shall find
Two together.
  God's grand design
Life unfolds with the
  Vows that bind.

A lucky day.
A lucky Dad.

4/12/81

Φ Φ Φ

A letter to my daughter, now the mother of three of my grandchildren and the baker of the bread.

To My Daughter:

-If you do no more than you have already accomplished in your young life--you will have surpassed my wildest dreams--

-You are a doer--a maker of life--Josh, Ariel and Rachael are proof positive. It's one thing to have a child, to love a child-- it's something special to mold a child in your best visions and traits, and it is even more to season that mold with the best of your partner----

-You have imbued your family with your excitement of life-- the hunger of a child for more and more learning--all without pressure or push--the excitement of "*which earring shall I wear*"--the little boy '*who had to be made to sit next to his teacher*'--three thinking machines who have taken Howard's brain power, mixed it with yours --and who each have a prod-uct that will surpass the '*givers*'.

-What prompted this note?
The reading of your '*CV*'--
The excitement of the list of credits--the thrill of '*familiar words and thoughts*'--Your mother passing by, preparing dinner--Good, warm, throbbing thoughts--

-So be it--you have indeed made your way and the peak lies just around the bend--

-We have lots of memories, you and I, and the "*little ones*"--

Very precious memories that will often soften the load of the day, if we let them--

1990

Getting to Know Them

One of the wisest decisions of my life was to vacation with my family; first my children and then my grandchildren, always with my wife. I found the opportunity to get o know my family. Bits of verse were often written to the kids!

To: Art and Gail

I look at my children and
    what do I see?
The best bits of mother and
    Some bits of me.

Good bits, other bits, their physics
    And their wits,
In their laughter, their charms, and
    Sometimes their fits!

But whatever they have got,
    No one can deny,
They are proof positive,
    I can never die!

12/29/90

Φ Φ Φ

Art

Many are the wonders of just
        Being a *'Dad'*,
Making of memories, the best
        You ever had.

When a child describes father,
        No jesting for the while,
As a *'shoulder to lean on'*,
        That says it all, my child.

For is that not just what, a
        Parent is really meant to be?
Not *'playmate'* or a *'go-fer'*,
        But a hand of security.

                12/89

            Φ Φ Φ

Gail

To be told that she is caring,
    Can be said of my every child.
When her son, Josh, happily describes her,
    He first describes her smile.

***

The bread she bakes is legend,
    At creative math she is a whiz.
She even plays the part of mother
    To three *easy to raise* kids.

***

One of her biggest problems,
    Is that she she so little to do.
Aerobics, shopping or writing,
    She's our daughter, tried and true.

12/89

Φ Φ Φ

The Family Grew

As my family grew, there came Robin and Howard. How fortunate we are to see them take their places alongside our children as life partners.

Robin
Howard

The working together that real
    Life demands.
Just being the one who always
    Understands.
The sharing of troubles, then wiping
    Our tears.

A haven to rest on, to set aside
    Fears.
How blessed are we all, that you are
    A part,
Both son and daughter, with a place
    In our heart.

12/29/90

Φ Φ Φ

A Toy Store

Shortly after my son married Robin, we attended a small dinner party at the newly-weds' home. Some of our dearest friends were present. After dinner, we sat around and discussed the experiences of married life. We went around the room and each person talked. The Blounts, the Ivey's, my wife, and I, and then it was Robin's turn.

She hesitated for a moment, looked around the room at all that Art had assembled as mementos of travel and time. She said that in her life amongst all new things and new experiences made her feel as though "I live in a toy store."

Robin

She's a swimmer and a home-maker
and she is even more.
I'll never forget her saying that
She "*lives in a toy store.*"

When she sells, or she rebels, and
She always stands her ground.
She's more than a peddler,
As many antique dealers have found.

But above all else, this girl of ours,
Is wedded to our son.
Indeed the hearts of all those
Who know her, are hearts she has won.

12/89

Φ Φ Φ

The Conference

Before I wrote these '89 verses about our new children, I gathered my grandchildren and had a conference. I asked them to describe their parents. I wrote what they said.

Howard

The most endearing precious words
    Known to man,
Are words from a child,
    As a child understands.

He is *'patient'* and he's *'nice'*,
    They called him *'loving,'* too.
They said he's *'fun to be with'*;
    That's how they described you.

No words of mine can better
    Or make the meaning more,
For not only do they love you,
    You're the one who they adore.

Φ Φ Φ

All the Wonderful Grandchildren

To Jennie

You know how I am when
    I'm tired and haven't
    had my rest
My attitudes just run amuck
    I'm truly not at my best

My tongue gets sharp
    And wild words flow
Why I do it, I will never know

My father also suffers
    From this uncontrolled disease
But after rest our own very sweet selves
    Come forth and try to please

                12/30/87

Φ Φ Φ

Jennie

In our lives there came a special thing
Cuddly and soft, with a voice of spring.
I held her close from the very first days.
I watched her grow and I loved her ways.

She was the very first, a little bit of me,
With a way with words and what a memory!
A clone of her mother and lots of her dad,
Bits of the best that both of them had.

I promise to see her not as a child
But a grown young lady wily and wild;
Free with her mind and all grown up,
No longer a baby, no longer a pup.

1/2/88

Φ Φ Φ

Jennie

Watch her playing checkers,
    You think you've won the day--

When suddenly, no warning,
    She makes her daring play.

You ask, "*What happened?*"
    As she takes your chips away.

Grown to be a lady,
    With an ever-growing heart

It's just good knowing that
    In her life we play a part.

1/1/89

Φ Φ Φ

Jennie

Not long ago, when I used to say,
To a little girl who came our way
"So big!, so big! you are this very day."

And now the years, over half a score,
Have flown by, a babe you are no more,
But a grown lady, I still adore!

12/29/90

Φ Φ Φ

To Sarah

I'm an independent person
    Who likes it done '*my way*.'
My heart is soft and tender
    And I really love to play.

Now when I get caught at doing,
    Things I should not do,
I close my eyes and close my ears,
    It's no use feeling blue.

But though I'm rough and ready
    And my name should be ' *Spike*',
I share, I care, I'm a happy one,
    Just a lovable little ' *Tyke*.'

              12/30/87

Φ Φ Φ

My Birthday Girl

This is to my Sarah
        She's a treasure and a joy,
Sometimes a dress-up little girl,
        Sometimes a wild tomboy,

She's six-years old, my Sarah,
        Going on twenty-five,
Quiet for a moment
        But so very much alive.

And she'll always be my Sarah
        With her tender little heart,
Walking with me where'er I go
        Playing her very special part.

                    1/22/88

                Φ Φ Φ

Sarah

Just where did you find it?
    Just where does the secret lie
That built such tenacity with
    Everything you try.

What other seven-year old lady,
    That anyone knows,
Wants only originals in her
    Crystals and her clothes?

With all of her collections,
    Her special touch of class,
Will her true love for the Joker
    Truly, really last?

12/89

Φ Φ Φ

Sarah

Sophistication, in cool control,
    She saves her pennies, so I am told,
Delights in the crystal that she can hold.

She knows what she wants and how to wait.
    If she has mind to she can relate.
You can't trick her, no matter the bait.

                        12/29/90

              Φ Φ Φ

69

Her Birthday Card -

Sarah

She loves the crystal's sparkle
   And she knows the good ones, too--

No one will ever fool her, even
   If they might fool you--

Perky little lady, our own
   Little bunny foo foo--

With her little dancing legs and
   hips--

Missing two front teeth between
   Her rosy lips.

1/1/89

Φ Φ Φ

To Rachael

Dresden is fine china,
    Its lines are straight and bold.
They say I resemble china
    But I'm only five-years old.

I'm hungry to know all the words
    That live in pages of each book;
To learn all of my numbers,
    No matter how long it took.

But I don't want to be like china
    Or any any other dish,
I want to be like my mother
    That truly is my wish.

12/30/87

Φ Φ Φ

Rachael

"*Snap*" goes her mind, she's
   Caught another thought;

Learning things by chance,
   Finding things she sought;

Loves the pretty dresses her
   Mother bought.

In her dancing, or her prancing,
   She's a hummer.

Marching to the tune of, a
   Different drummer.

1/1/88

Φ Φ Φ

Rachael

What have you learned this
      Year gone by?
What special adventures
      Did you try?

It's grown up books that
      You now enjoy.
Is it true you also
      Kiss a boy?

How grown-up can
      Your seven years be?
Already you're years
      Ahead of me!

12/89

Φ Φ Φ

Rachael

Never before have I seen
        Such a child!
Whose manner is often less
        Than mild,
Learning, life, logic, in her
        Mind filed.

She is a dozen steps ahead of me.
The oldest child of a lively three.
Pray tell me, what is her destiny?

                        12/29/90

            Φ Φ Φ

(After her participating in 'Odyssey of the Mind')

Rachael

Not for Winnin',

Not for Losin',

Just for Being

And for Choosin'

To try your wits.

Forget the fits

In somethin' new

Can Do! Can Do!

2/29/92

Φ Φ Φ

Ariel

I've come to the conclusion
    Because I think it's true,
That you must have a wiggly worm
    Living inside of you.

It wiggles when you try to nap
    Like something I've never seen;
Arms twist, legs turn, this a-way, that a-way
    That worm is surely mean.

It doesn't let you find a place
    Just to lay and rest,
Squirms and rolls your little self
    But that worm gives you zest.

Take care of that little worm
    Let it have its whirl.
That same little wiggly worm
    Your mother knew, when she
        Was a little girl.

12/20/87

Φ Φ Φ

Ariel

A little bit of sunshine
      When sunshine's needed most.

She always plays the hostess
      No matter who's the host.

Just how did she learn so very
      Much to say?

Perpetual motion, both night
      And day.

She's got her own very special,
      Special way.

                              1/1/89

            Φ Φ Φ

Ariel

What stories you always have
　　　To tell!
Why is it you must always
　　　Rebel?
Your sure-fire, snap-trap mind
　　　Makes me *'Kvell'*.

How to charm, to cuddle and to kiss.
You touch my heart, my very little Miss.
Where indeed did you learn
　　　All of this?

　　　　　　　12/29/90

　　　Φ Φ Φ

Josh

Walk me, hold me, don't ever
   Put me down,
Unless I let you know
   I want to hit the ground.

Forget trying to make me sleep
   There's too much life to see.
Just find the strength of ten good men
   So you can take care of me.

And when I get so restless
   That it isn't my best day,
Just hold your tongue and to me
   Never sharp things say.

No matter how I try you
   And weary work your arms,
Just watch me when I wake from sleep
   I'm a bundle of little charms!

12/20/87

Φ Φ Φ

Josh

This a-way and that a-way,
   Just tell me what should I do.

You don't even have to ask him,
   For he'll soon be telling you.

A '*Godfather*' in the making
   And the kid is only 'two'!

                    1/1/89

Φ Φ Φ

Josh

The light in the room gets brighter.
The load on my back gets lighter.
The ties of my heart grow tighter.

As all here assembled were once told,
We're watching you grow, you fit the mold.
Our little leader, now four years old.

                    12/29/90

Φ Φ Φ

A Winter Fall

It was a winter day with ice and snow, so we sat with the family and reminisced about the time Bea, my wife, slipped and fell in the driveway, suffering a skull fracture.

We started to leave the three-year old Josh insisted that he walk us to our car.

Josh

My little man, my little man,
    So much of life you understand.

Mom told you the story of
    Mom-Mom's falling on the ice.
Your caring heart then told you
    That that could not happen twice.

While all your cousins were playing,
    As children like to play,
Precious you just had to leave them
    To help us on our way.

You had to walk beside us,
    No matter the winter snow.
And I could not reason why
    My boy would not let us go.

You could not leave your Mom-Mom,
    Yet you had to stand by me,
And all the while your Pop-Pop,
    He was just too blind to see.

I sent you back to the house,
    Your eyes were filled with tears.
I yelled at my precious boy,
    Wise far beyond his years.

You've touched our hearts in many a way,
But never as much as you did that day.

              12/89

Φ Φ Φ

*To entertain my grandchildren, I
reduced several famous parables to verse*

Steady But Slow

Turtle
Said the Turtle to the Hare,
"Betcha I can beat you there
Cause I'm steady tho' I'm slow
I get where I want to go!"

Hare
"I am made with spice and speed
My legs move without the need
of any effort on my part
All I have to do is start!"

Turtle
"That may be true," Hare heard
"But you'd stop along the road,
I'm steady, I never stop
Until I reach mountain's top!"

Hare
"Don't make me laugh !" rabbit said,
"I could spend the day in bed.
Let you start before the dawn
Let you crawl thru' woods and faun.

However far thought you went
However you tried and spent
I would pass you on the way
And win the race every day!"

Turtle
"Enough! time's wasting for me
Let's get started, then we'll see.
Anyone can boast, snort and shout
Really, what it's all about?"

Laughing Hare then sped ahead.
Turtle moved like he's dead.
Full speed .. soon wore the Hare out.
Puffing he looked about.

Hare
Turtle was nowhere in sight.
Hare laughed at Turtle's plight.
"Guess I'll stop and rest awhile."
Thoughts of Turtle made Hare smile.

Hare fell into a deep sleep,
Never knowing just how deep.
While Turtle thumped his way,
Not talking, he'd had his say.

Darkness fell and Hare slept on.
Turtle just thumped with scorn.
Then behold! Turtle passed.
He knew boasters never last.

Finish line was just ahead,
When Hare got up from his bed.
Galloping off without doubt,
That he would yet win this bout.

But little did the Hare know
Turtles move steady, slow,
Lo and behold, the very end
Just around the next road bend.

Hare moved with a Hare's speed.
Turtle groped without heed,
To where Hare was or had been.
Turtle knew he would yet win.

Finish line was thin and tight.
Turtle ran with all his might.
Hare sighted the finish line.
Turtle thought, that line is mine.

He was at the stopping place.
Could it be, he won the race?
Hare sped by with lightning speed.
Turtle's neck shot out indeed!

Ribbon tore against Hare's breast.
All his speed but he's second best.
With neck jumping from the shell,
Turtle rang the winner's bell!

Φ Φ Φ

The Hummingbird Said

Somewhere I have read
That the hummingbird said
"I can fly higher than you!"
With a glint in his eye
They heard eagle reply
"That's something you'll never do!"
So they both took a stand
The eagle so grand
The hummingbird, tiny but true.

"Then let's have a race
You name time and place
We'll see what each can do!"
"Why not here and now"
Hummingbird said, *"Pal,*
I'll race you up to the sun!"
The eagle did smile
"I'll win by a mile
This race is already won!"

As he spread each wing
You could hear the birds sing
"This is a sight fit for song!"
His head he held high
His eyes in the sky
And away he flew mighty and strong.

All the birds searched the ground
Hummingbird couldn't be found
"Guess he was frightened away!"
The birds searched and searched
Under branches and birch
And the things you heard them say!

*"We heard the hummingbird lie!
He should be banned from the sky!
His honor and pride has burst!"*

***

Wise owl just sat high
With a glint in his eye
"Let the race be over first!"

***

Eagle strained muscle and limb
No hummingbird could outfly him
He flew until he could no further go.

"I've won this day!"
The eagle did say
As softly he stared below

***

They say he heard
A sound so absurd
That the thing just couldn't be!

***

For high over his head
Wings fluttered and spread
Hummingbird said
"Look up at me!"

He said with a grin
*"Just where have you been
I'm tired of waiting for you!"*

***

Yes, hummingbird won
The impossible, had been done
The little bird was highest of the two!

***

In the dark of the night
When few birds take flight
Wise owl sat high on a limb

***

*"Come hummingbird, tell me true
The race is over, what did you do
To outwit eagle, to outsmart him!*

"I'm so little and light
That for most of the flight
I hid on his back feathered bed

***

And when he was spent
Off I gently went
And flew high above his head!"

Wise owl winked his eye,
He now understood why,
Hummingbird had won from the start.

***

Races lost can often be won
Will it and it can be done.
The secret is use of head and heart!

Dedicated to Jennifer

Φ Φ Φ

Birth

The womb is torn and rid of strife
The babe is born, a spawn of life,
The eyes are closed,
The lips are sealed,
The mind disposed,
The wound is healed.
The babe lives on,
And grows to know
The dusk-the dawn
The touch of woe.
The mother's breast, her heart and soul
Gives out her best, her babe to hold.
The infant then, so tenderly
Turns about and tries to see.
It alights and whines and clutters close,
It sights and finds one it loves most,
It speaks with sound of new born bliss;
For delight it's found in the mother's kiss.

May, 1942

Φ Φ Φ

Her Little Son

Each evening when the dusk appears,
The soft night draws away all fears
As a mother sheds those joyful tears--
    For her little son.

Asleep he lies there in his bed,
His guardian angel at his head;
For he is the life of this homestead--
    Her little son.

He'll dream of when he's grown to be
A sailor man and gone out to sea,
A general like Grant or Lee--
    Her little son.

He'll dream of riding the clouds above
And the fairy princess he'll grow to love;
Yes, these are the things which he'll dream of--
    Her little son.

And as the dawn brings forth its light,
He'll rise and go about his plight;
He'll play favor in his mother's sight--
    This little son.

The many things which he will do-
He'll fill book pages full of glue;
He'll stop the clock and spoil the stew--
    Her little son.

She'll call aside her pride and joy
And speak a word to this little boy;
Then take away that best playtoy--
    From her little son.

But however harsh are the words she'll say,
In her heart she'll hate to stop his play;
And for every tear, oh, how she will pay--
    Poor little son.

Yet, she must not let him fight,
She must explain the wrong from right;
That truth shines through the dark of night--
    To her little son.

So that when he's older and grown tall,
He'll often look back and see it all;
The wisdom in her every call--
    Her little son.

And until the day she's put to rest,
She'll ever gain the pride and zest;
To guide through life one she loves best--
    Her little son.

Dedicated to Barry Stevens
March 1942

Φ Φ Φ

A Maternal Aunt Lost A Newborn Boy At Birth

Keep Faith

Strange indeed is this God of ours,
I often fear his mighty powers,
As mortals we have seen His wrath,
Destroy at will all man made craft.

You my friends have known too,
The countless things our God can do,
You, more so, than other men,
Have felt His might strike time again.

Perhaps when most you felt the pain,
You dared to think your prayers in vain,
And turned aside with hearless ears,
To blot out all your Godly fears.

With His sight, as only God can see,
Some days ago He took from thee,
What might have been a healthy son,
Or by chance a far less fortunate one.

His mercy looked down upon,
The parents of that lifeless son,
And with His grace there and then,
He gave you a son again.

A son who will grow to be,
A man of unknown destiny,
And thru the years your boy will stride,
To fill your hearts with a parent's pride.

Never permit your bitterness,
No matter how deep your distress,
To daunt your trust in God above,
Or foul the reverence of Godly love.

To Uncle Ben
12/22/42

Φ Φ Φ

A Letter to my Little Girl

The thought has grown in my mind as to why I did not write you at least one letter during this past year at school.

Was it because I was too preoccupied with the pressures of the day? This was not the reason.

Was it because I saw you almost every weekend, or that I knew your mother wrote you so often? These were not the reasons.

Was it because I loved you less or that I cared less? You, in your little heart so full of love and emotion, know this was not the reason.

I could say and be to a great extent true, that it was because I have so much confidence and faith in your sense of right and wrong and in your ability to perform, that you did not need the written word. These words though expressing my deepest feelings only partially answer the question *"Why?"*

The whole truth is that I don't know the reason *"Why?"*

It is now the early morning hours. I have been reading; your mother sleeps. The book I read motivated me to write. It tells me that I lost an opportunity in not writing. It tells me, or better yet, it reminds me for I, of all people, should never forget what joy a letter brings.

Your father is a very happy man. He has perhaps more than he deserves.

As I recall the many things I have done in life that I would do or I should have done differently one fact stands out above all others. Never in any moment of sanity have I lost faith in the strength of my God. Because He has blessed me as he has, I <u>KNOW</u> that He expects no perfection from man or woman. I <u>KNOW</u> that he views the whole of life of a man or a woman and sheds upon them His tests of strength and endurance, of patience and of the acceptance of success of failure; and that He judges not the hour nor the day <u>but the life</u>.

You have brought into my life great beauty and love. You have been blessed with great wisdom. You are a source of never ending pride to both your parents.

Learn well!

Believe the best of all your grow to know but remember *"perfection in man or woman is the proper proportion of imperfections."*

The story of the taking of a skirt is but part of the story. Great tragedy can affect different people differently. Rebellion against the establishment is neither all right nor is it all wrong. We all need guidance no matter how old we grow. I certainly need it now more than at any other time of my life.

If God sees fit not to judge the man or the woman until the end of their days do not judge too harshly any single act or any group of acts of anyone whom you now love or one whom you will grow to love.

Your tomorrow, my little girl, is to be full of all the passions and beauties of life. You, who have so much love to give, will find that love generates love and all you give will be returned many fold. Your tomorrows will reap as mine have reaped, the rich love of children, of a mate and of parents.

As I write, you are asleep only a few doors away. I could perhaps tell you all these things and many things more. I thought perhaps you might prefer a letter.

From your daddy
who loves you
because
you are you

Dad

8/1/69

*To My Daughter and Her Betrothed
on Their Wedding Day on a Rainy Day*

Rain

Rain is the fluid of life, it
    Causes the bulbs of the tulip
    To bloom-
Without the bloom of the tulip-
    How dull life would be-
With God's rain flows all the
    Best of good fortune-
May all your life together
    Always know the drops of
    Rain that give birth to
    Growing things

Φ Φ Φ

Baby

Ten little fingers, ten little toes,

Quivering lips and a perky nose.

Someone to hold me, someone to care.

"Lift me up gently." Lots of love there!

Once you cuddle and hold baby close,

The ties that that matter, will bind you most.

Φ Φ Φ

My Child

True answers I may never know, although
    I can now see more clear.
It's in times of stress of those I love, they
    become to me most ' *dear*'.

I feel their pain, I know their doubts and
    their uncertainties I share.
When they are sick in heart or sore of
    limb, it's then that I most care.

Φ Φ Φ

Baby Tears

The tear that flows from baby faces
In my land or in distant places
Spells out the world that will come to be
For what is good for them is good for me.

1982

Φ Φ Φ

Vision of Peace

A vision came to a child at sleep.
Of a land where lions played with sheep;
Of a time and a place free from fears
Oh God of Peace may that day be near.

1983

Φ Φ Φ

Mother's Breast

God's new born babe safely rests
On soft mounds of mother's breasts
What better sign can men see
Of God's peace and tranquility.

1984

Φ Φ Φ

The Little Ones

Excited voices fill the air,
 Precious sounds of glee,
Waving arms, curly hair,
 Are waiting there for me.

Words of joy, words of cheer,
 Sparking a happy tear,
A child's words so very dear,
 "Someone we love is here!"

Just to have a child say,
 "Grandma you've been away!"
Just to close eyes and see,
 The child brings love to me.

This is how life should be spent,
 This is how life should be seen,
To treasure each moment lent,
 This is how I live my dream.

   9/25/86
   "Plane from London"

 Φ Φ Φ

Lessons

These are the truths I must my children
        teach
That the best of live lives within their reach.

That no matter how bitter life may seem
Precious peace of mind lives within each dream.

Search your heart my child, and there you
        will find
Those very means that bring you your peace of
        mind.

Each life you knew, indeed, played its part
Memories relived in your tender heart.

My child, lessons of life are mine to give
But only you can make the lessons live.

Φ Φ Φ

HOSPITAL

I Went to the Hospital

It was a long ride to the hospital,
To make it in fifteen minutes seemed impossible.
I was sleeping, and so
When I got there I did not know.

It felt the same all the way to me,
And I didn't know where I could be.
Doctors all over the room were spread.
Looking at me while I was in bed.

At last night came,
And all was the same,
Except the nurses, who were changed,
And the room special she had it arranged.

The night nurse was one of the best,
For she was different from some of the rest.
Her time to work was in the night,
And she tried to help the patients with all her might.

At last morning came
And everything was the same.
Another nice nurse was Mrs. Rush,
Who never told the children to hush.

But to others it was such a chatter,
Which to me did not matter.
And if you ever go to a hospital,
Go to Sydenham if possible.

11 years old
1933

Φ Φ Φ

Got the word your tail's a-draggin'--
    Hope that soon you're up and waggin'!

Tho' it's a known fact, and a certain cure
    The pain is much more than you dare endure

That an apple a day keeps doc away
    But what can you do if the Doc is Jay?

                    2/17/87

      Φ Φ Φ

INSPIRATION

Thoughts Related to Inspiration

Even the most vowed optimist is subject to pessimistic thought-The negative thought begets further negative thought-

The distinction between the pessimist and the optimist comes with the optimist control of thought trend. Just as the optimist knows that positive thought begets positive thought and negative thought begets negative thought he forcibly finds the positive

10/79

Limitations

There are those who grab the reins
of life and drive them to the hilt,
Sometimes they run a winning race,
Sometimes they trip and tilt.

What matters most is that they tried,
Lost and tried again,
It's the trying to test one's fate,
That marks the best of men.

Should one know what cannot be done,
Never daring past his scope,
Or soar beyond all limits set, and build
A life on hope?

Φ Φ Φ

Heeding

It is well to know the great who live,
The saints who have had so much to give.

The giants who soared above the earth,
Thinkers from whom new ideas gave birth.

Reading the deeds of those who dared.
Hearing voices of those who cared.

But to what avail if with it all,
I fail to heed or hear their call?

Φ Φ Φ

Turn the Failure

The line that divides success and failure
    Is thinner than a hair.
We are often standing on top of it,
    Not knowing we are there!
When with a touch of patience and pushin
    That little extra bit.
One can turn the failure, making
    A glorious success of it!

Φ Φ Φ

Highway

Watch the highway, wide and straight,
Watch the drivers test their fate.
Fly the road and cross the lane,
Cross right and then left again.

So alike the road of life,
Full of struggle, full of strife,
If you drive straight and true,
What in life can you not do?

1986

Φ Φ Φ

Head-On

Whenever the trials of life hit you or me,

Remember the wisdom of the ship at sea.

Don't run, don't hide, you must never turn away.

Sail the waves head-on into a calmer day.

1988

Φ Φ Φ

The ability to make decisions is often lacking in many of us. I view the process as the Balance Scale of Justice, one can reason why they should or why they should not. The secret is to weigh the facts and suppositions, just so far and decide. Then make it work.

Decision

Don't stack all weights of judgment
    on life's balance scale
Weigh pros and cons, but let your sense
    of ought prevail.

The secret is decisions sometimes
    quickly made
Are better than not deciding 'fore
    visions fade.

If never seen, how can you tell which
    road is best?
If never seen, how can you tell which
    path winds less?

Is it not better to travel the
    bumpy road,
Then to be full of seed that you
    never sowed?

When you wait till you are certain of
    what is right
Doing nothing is the cruel price paid
    for your plight.

I am telling you because I have
    found it so
You must weigh the facts just so far and
    let it go.

Φ Φ Φ

Secrets

The secrets of a better life are as near to
   us as breath itself;

---From Ancient Greeks, the starting point,
   KNOW THYSELF

---Think POSITIVE for it is certain,
   POSITIVE THOUGHT begets
   POSITIVE THOUGHT

---Grow by giving of yourself to cause and
   Country

---Recognize the force of life WITHIN YOU,
   it can move mountains

---KNOW THYSELF, for as you think so
   will you be.

                 1976

Φ Φ Φ

May it Soon Be

May the days ahead bring...

---Peace to all nations,...Peace of Mind
   to all mankind;

---Even strides to walk beyond the
   frustrations of life;

---Abundance of health of body and
   health of spirit;

---Concern of all men for the welfare
   of every man's child;

---Enthusiasm for living in a land where
   men are free.

Φ Φ Φ

True Sharing

"Most exciting day of my life!" she said.
This lady of character well born and bred.

"Today my platelets I hope to donate,
To my friend whose need is so truly great.

"The excitement of giving part of me
Sharing what God has allowed to be

"It's like having another share my sight
How can such sharing be other than right?"

11/90

Φ Φ Φ

Measure Your Wealth

Measure your wealth by the intangibles of life as well as by man made material values. Draw a line down the center of a blank page. Title side one "*Wealth of Hand*," and title side two "*Wealth of Heart*." First list your accounts on one side as these are material values, the accepted values of trade and finance. The list contains cash on hand, stocks, bonds, properties and other investments. This portion of your balance sheet can be audited by any stranger and its accuracy proved or disproved. These are cold facts.

Move to side two of the sheet, a warmer climate. To list intangibles requires thought, thinking of values often overlooked. Ask yourself "*what accepted values can I list here*?" For a moment you ponder in disgust. What are the values of the heart? You think and for a time your pen refuses to move. Then you slowly touch the sheet and the pen begins to show life. You list real intrinsic values.

List your mind. You have a mind, it is an intangible. List '*Faith*,' faith in God and faith in man. List the tenderness of love and devotion. List the beauty of memory, memories of a woman's warmth, of a mother's voice, of the laughter of youth. Search further and find more. Touch upon the happiness of your home. You remember tears and strangely enough you now know that tears themselves, when caused by another's concern over your well-being, are an unmeasurable asset. List the passing personalities of your life, parents, heroes, adolescent loves. You add words of compound meanings, happiness and pride. You find your sheet is short and so you take another.

You think of the values around you, not feelings or moods but the living values that you can see but that you cannot touch. You list the sunshine and the freshness of the air. You list the giants of nature, the forests and the waterfalls; you also list the infinite charms of nature, the gold of a buttercup and the ting of a drop of rain. You write on and on and on, and with the more you write, the wealthier you become. You list health and the blessings of a sound body. You realize that no upper total can compare to the lower total, that no monetary wealth can compensate for the strength of life. It becomes clear there is wealth within the reach of every man. You know that no amount of dollars can buy a mother's love for her child, or a man's deep rooted faith in the unknown.

8/5/48

φ φ φ

PAIN

Making Man

When God began to make this world,
　　Mid skies aglow with sunlight,
He planned as He molded man, then
　　He made both day and night.

"Creating woman, creating man,
　　Upright I'll make them stand,
The very best of My master plan,
　　This is good. This is grand."

He watched with pride, the man He made,
　　Then salted life with stress,
God said aloud, *"It is good I see,*
　　Now put them to the test."

He spoke as He reviewed His work,
　　He said, *"That's not enough,*
I'll salt this man with much aches, and pain,
　　To really make him tough."

Why give man pain? I've often asked,
　　Why make the heart know tears?
Why pass to man, throughout all his days,
　　Life's tragedies and fears?

128

When I was young, I asked these things,
　　I never understood,
Could plights of man, famines, wars or hate,
　　Come from a God so good?

The halfway point of life has passed,
　　The years go spinning by,
An older mind, a seasoned heart,
　　Still seek the reason why.

11/22/76

Φ Φ Φ

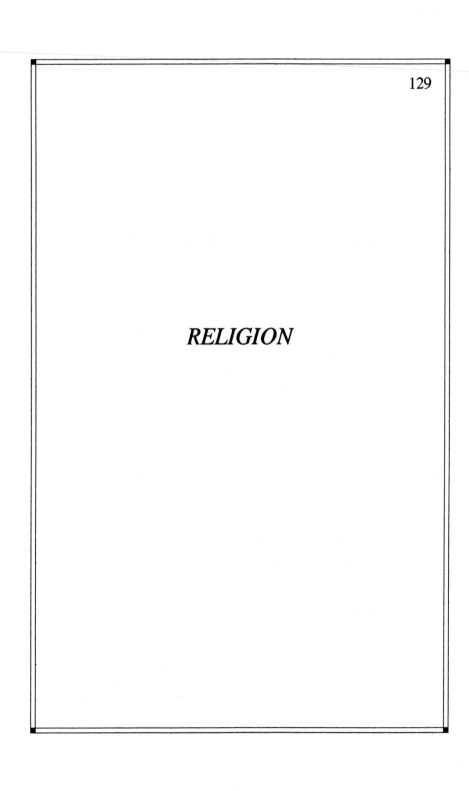

RELIGION

The Design

Each of us is a part of history, not by choice but by design. To be born, to know life are in themselves a part of history. The living being partakes of all the life experiences of his or her parents, each of whom in turn is part of the life experience of their parents. This heritage goes back <u>ad infinitum,</u> traits that seem to disappear in one generation often glow in a new life in a generation skipped. How often have you seen the strength or stamina of a grandparent skip the child and live again in the grandchild?

Our heritage, our ties to yesteryear, are not accident, they are design.

Life is man's part in the partnership of creation. To have been born or to have given birth is each person's act in the partnership of creation. Life is holy. The act of creating life is holy. It is part of the design.

These beliefs were in my mind during all of my adult life. The proof of the promise came with my presence in Israel, the Holy Land.

March, 1983

Φ Φ Φ

The Jew

"*Who are these Jews? And tell me why?*
I should care if they live or die?

Throughout the ages leaders have said,
"*It may be best if they were dead!*"

"*God's my witness, he surely knows*
I would not use my sword or blows."

"*What can I do if men defy,*
How they live and the way they die?

"*The way they pray, the way they dance*
Flaunt their learning, their haughty prance."

"*Don't they cause all our worldly ills,*
The cause of the plague that kills?"

"*They bring on themselves the plights they know,*
To keep our peace, they have to go!"

"*Jews are not wanted in any land.*
Where can they go? What's the world's plan?"

I asked myself, will it last?
Will all futures be like the past?

Φ Φ Φ

Broken Promises

It's You who guides the wisdom of the
    tenets of our creed,
It is You who truly knows the depth of our
    every need.

You are not swayed by fancy, You know no
    vanity,
You project what is the best part of life
    served by we.

Yet how often have we not heard the roaring
    of Your winds?
How often have You sighed at the folly of
    our sins?

I, just like all men, have tested You; time
    and time again;
With my thoughts, my dreams, wasted
    moments I so often spend,

Promises we have made You, promises that
    we failed to keep.
Promises made when hearts are heavy, when
    eyes are bound to weep.

For once the pain passes and the grief is
    no longer there;
We rationalize away the promises, the
    causes, the care.

How often we see moonbeams though
    the moon is hid from view
And yet we know the moon is there,
    lighting the skies for You.

With each breath, each moment, and
    every movement of the air.
Though I have never seen You, I truly
    know You are there.

Φ Φ Φ

The Congregation
What Does this Sanctuary Mean

So many circles of life we see
Each etched into our memory,

Here where our child took a marriage vow;
Kaddish said for those not with us now,

Confirmation and Bar Mitzvah day;
A grandchild on her Bat Mitzvah way,

The proud naming of a new born babe,
The solace a mourning heart will crave,

Opening the Torah, let the Scroll talk.
The touch and kiss of the Torah walk.

Those stirring moments, heart touching times,
Jew to Jew sharing a fate that binds.

The fearless voices of far sighted men,
Oh! The need to hear them speak again!

Compassion and caring!
Bold vision and daring!

5/13/92

Φ Φ Φ

NATURE

The Wondrous Lily

Amid a growing crowd of roses
With honor bold, the lily poses,
Perched upon the fruitful ground,
Petals loftily looking down.
Swaying gently with the breeze,
Accompanied by loving swarms of bees,
Rocking nobly in the air,
Guarding the willow's precious lair.
Head perched high, tipped slender stem,
Toward the sky the leaflets bend,
Sunbeams glow in relentless bloom,
Commending lily to her watchful doom.

1937

Φ Φ Φ

Cut the Tree Down

I saw a man take ax in hand
    and kill a tree that stood.
Falling, I heard it say, "*I am*
    more than a piece of wood!"

"*My many roots have bound the land*
    and held the slope in tow,
The shade I gave; the fruit of my brow
    will now never grow."

"*It is now your choice.*" The tree said,
    "*I cannot fight your whim.*"
"*I know that man's saw and ax are not*
    the best part of him."

What caught my blinking eye when
    I next saw the fallen tree,
Was a strip of bark tied to its trunk
    making a last plea.

What magic sustenance passed thru'
    that splintered tie?
What strange power gave proof that
    the tree just didn't want to die?

On that dying trunk a flower blossomed,
    a true life sign,
What lesson does this symbol mean to
    be both yours and mine?

The moral of this story and its every
    word is true.
Is that we should hold onto life
    whatever else we do.

1991

Φ Φ Φ

Talking Tree

The acorn is the beginning, the giant
    oak is the end.
Thru' winds and storms and droughts,
    somehow great oaks never bend.

Their limbs may sway and stutter,
    occasionally limbs fall.
But proud oaks reach above me and
    seem to withstand it all.

"Let nature prune my leaves and limbs,
    And tear dead wood away.
But my deep roots hold me steady even
    though my trunk may sway."

"What are the lessons of growing, needed
    to reach this end?
As a young sprout I knew my lot
    and with the winds I'd bend."

"Life's secret-it's the will that counts, the
    will that surely sees;
The vastness all about me; the living
    beyond us trees!"

"To compass I'm a beacon. The tip of my
highest brow,
Is a sighting point for strangers, who seem
to know somehow."

"That if they never lose sight of the very
top of my head.
No matter how they drift and fall or flounder
in their stead."

"If they walk the line that leads them to
where my deep roots start.
They will find their way in darkness if they
never lose heart."

So it is with the life we lead,
however it began.
Have a goal and hold your goal, don't you
be an *"Also-Ran!"*

Φ Φ Φ

While on a photographic Safari, traveling from Nairobi to Mombasa, Africa and back, experiencing the living with nature's wonders, this verse was written.

Jambo

Jambo greets you along the way
Adult and child all proudly say
Jambo-Jambo means "How are you?"

The people make a Country great,
The people seal a Country's fate.
A happy people, free from hate
And free from fear in Kenya State.

The smiling faces on every man
Greet the traveler in this land.
"We'll be happy to see you when
Rundi Tena, come back again!"

10/30/85

Φ Φ Φ

For several days we rode elephants thru the Nepal jungle hunting tiger. Everything gets out of the elephants' way. Rhinos who charge four wheel vehicles walk out of the elephant's path.

Elephant

An elephant sails through the jungle,
Just plodding along his way.
The scents and cries about him
Neither bother his work or his play.

If the camel is the ship of the desert;
The whale is the king of the sea;
Elephant admiral of the jungle,
Say "*Hello*" to his majesty.

Ever atop an elephant,
    riding to and fro?
Going wherever the king
    decided to go.
Stopping as he pulled choice greens
    from both tree and ground.
Storing food, trunk to mouth, all
    the stalks he found.

Walking slow and steady,
    always in command.
Tolerating on his back,
    A woman and a man.
"*No hurry, no worry, remember
    all is well.*

Elephant eats most jungle greens,
His mouth holds what he pulls with his trunk.
Devours the sprouts that are choice,
Without fan fare spits out the junk.

The elephant baby is in training,
Learning to follow command.
The herd forms a wall to stop him,
When he runs away in the sand.

You can prod elephants thru the waters;
Thru streams that steady flow;
But don't prod them when they're thirsty;
For the king just refuses to go.

Rhino

We met the feeding Rhino
    its armor plate in tack,
Indeed I was happy, high up
    on elephant's back.
The feeding Rhino eyed us,
    while circling his ground;
Tolerating elephant; showing
    his judgment sound.
Ran off into high grass,
    out of sight.
He knew the jungle king,
    he knew its might.
"Might charge a jeep, or
    hit a Rover van.
Not any elephant carrying
    a man!"

Φ Φ Φ

The Eagle

The eagle rests on highest branch

Of a mighty jungle tree.

All the wild passes below him,

All the world is for him to see.

2/1988

Φ Φ Φ

From Katmandu in Nepal we traveled over the Himalayan mountains to Tiger Top and wrote of the jungle scenes.

Shangri-La

Search high, search low

Wherever you may go

And yes you will never find,

Magic lands of peace and wonder,

Shangri-La is the state of your mind.

Φ Φ Φ

Jungle Night

I rest beneath the oil lamp's light,
As these words of truth I slowly write.
Believe them next time you are told
That jungle nights can be very cold,

There are many sounds in the jungle,
Many calls of the wild;
Some are like the sounds of thunder;
Some are like the cries of a child.

Surprising just how steady this oil lamp can be.
Not a flicker or a quiver, plenty light for me.
Not knowing what delights the morrow may hold;
I must return to covers, my tale's not fully told.

2/1988

Φ Φ Φ

Tiger

There is little light in the jungle,
The moon is too far away,
But bold is the eye of the tiger,
He sees as though it was day.

Ahoy! They've spotted the tiger,
From the tracks so fresh below.
Ten elephants close in, form a circle.
Where did the tiger go?

For tiger track is a tiger
         track distinct in every way.
A deep imprint round and clear;
         indeed not out to play.
Headed for the water hole,
         was it to drink his fill?
Or did he softly stalk his
         very next nightly kill?

                    2/1988

              Φ Φ Φ

In native dug-outs we traveled the river. Never have I heard silence such as the silence all about us moving down the waters. On both banks crocodiles lay in the sands. We were told they only ate fish.

The Crock

Motionless crock lies on sandy shore.

And blends with the sands of the sea.

Waiting for whoever may wander by;

I hope it's not you or me!

Φ Φ Φ

In a native village I saw a straw look-out tower sitting high on stilts of bamboo. Each night children mount the tower---

Native Watch

Rhinos munching farmers' fields,

The rice is their delicacy.

Look-outs perched in blinds above,

Beat a drum, the rhinos flee.

Φ Φ Φ

A Wife's Bed

It was her choice as to who
    shares her bed.
Her words are still ringing
    in my head.
She said, *"I thank you for your*
    offer, I truly do,
But this water bottle's staying;
    there's not room for you."

When hearing of her groping in the
    dark of night,
Hunting, looking, feeling for her
    lost flashlight,
I quickly jumped to protect her
    from the wild,
"Stand safe," I shouted to her,
    "Fear not, my child!"

She was already covered,
    heard her snore,
Before my feet hit and raced
    across the floor.
But I was now awakened
    hearing jungle sounds;
The howling of jackals,
    the baying of the hounds.

I held the screams inside me
        biting back the pain.
The torture seemed to carry
        through my every vein.
I shined my trusty light and
        saw below;
The corner post had broken my
        every toe.

I hobbled into the head,
        the lamp was lit.
Gently touched my toe
        and examined it.
My brain caught my sign and
        sent out a call.
The toe jiggled, wiggled
        not broken at all.

Φ Φ Φ

TIME

Time Passes

Nothing is what it used to be,

    Places and persons, like you and me.

Of all these things time takes its toll.

    That which is young will soon grow old.

Brick and mortar all built by man,

    Like man, will turn to grains of sand.

Φ Φ Φ

Time Lost

Time does not pass me by

When it's lost, fault is I.

Dreams and hope never die.

Φ Φ Φ

Time Flies

No one knows,

Where times goes.

Does it fly?

Does it die?

Φ Φ Φ

PHILOSOPHY

160

At Age Fourteen---

Life

Life is like a book--it begins and it ends;
It has its turns, its joys and its bends.
Its introduction is when we are born.
To live a life to be shattered and torn;
And then, from a child up to a man,
We'll do the best we possibly can.
Little by little, part by part,
Up to the climax we shall dart.
We'll finish our education and throw
    away our toys
And then reach life's real worries
    and joys.
Then, little by little, hop by hop,
Down to the conclusion we shall drop.
And as we turn it page by page,
We gradually reach old age.
As I'll say, as I've said before
On my wonderful lifetime tour,
It begins when we are born and
    continues till we die--
Life itself is something impossible
    to buy.

1936

Φ Φ Φ

Grand Design

Could it just happen and then,
Happen over and over again.

Dark of night breeds light of dawn,
The sperm from which all new life is spawn.

Tree limbs always winter bare,
Flower anew with the warm spring air.

These thoughts must not leave the mind,
They are all part of the grand design.

1986

Φ Φ Φ

162

A Man and a Thought

The wind was blowing, the rain did pour,
The ruthless waves clashed upon a covered shore,
The heavens darkened 'til skies were black,
The lightning curled 'round the gaping shack,
The thunder roared and clashed in vain
To the steady harmony of the falling rain.
The winds blew with force unknown;
All men did quake with fear unshown;
Yet, there stood one among them all
Who stood amazed at the sights now seen
And thrilled with joy at nature's whining call.
He stood there manning with his senses keen.

"Alas," thought he while gazing aloft,
"Could the Mighty One be so tender and soft;
And yet in the gleam of the coming morn
Show remnants remaining of destruction so torn,
Cause sorrow, great fear and heavy remorse,
Bring shame and hate in His blundering course."
How frightful it seemed to this lone sorrowed man
To realize the power behind that one booming hand,
To sense with full feeling while making this stand
How vast yielding fields and cities so grand
Could become so suddenly devastated land.

But suddenly he realized while one hand did sway
What grace giving goodness the right hand could fray.
He thought for a moment then brilliantly spoke,
When aglow from the enchantment he so suddenly woke.

"To see this great madness extending so wide
Bring sad hearts such gladness approaching with pride;
Through the highways so ceaseless such events yea did glide
While the high hopes so reachless were meaningly spied.
Avast, thought he, still mooring the heavens,
What fools are we, blind, while the Lord beckons
Our souls to be stroked through with such meaning
That we readily see the need for not leaning
On the shoulders of another; but with much haste
Adjust our marred movements on which my theory is based."

Unto the world, these words the man did shout
Explaining the boredom from which this logic had sprout.

September, 1938

Φ Φ Φ

Success and Failure

It is said, and I have found it so;
Tho' often I've been too blind to know;
That sadness has happiness in tow.

Success and failure stand side by side.
Touching close, the success seems to hide
Behind the throes of one's foolish pride.

Parted by only a thin hair's thread
As close as the nodding of one's head.
The two lying in the very same bed.

Try patience '*just a little bit more*!'
Success alone is worth fighting for
Failure can turn to success for sure.

What is success? Not money or gain.
It's light of the sun, touch of the rain
The love of a friend, moments of pain.

It's welcoming life, absence of hell;
Sounds of '*Hello*!'; the ring of the bell;
Eye of the needle; it's point as well.

Behind all the pain, how can it be?
I look and I look. What do I see?
An '*inner peace*' waiting for you and me.

Φ Φ Φ

Dreams Lost

Just as certain that all that lives will soon be clay
The night may be dark but there is light with each day.

There were the daydreams that would often blind my sight,
And the dreams that flowed thru my being at night.

No matter what the price life extracted from me,
I knew, I just knew, what I was going to be.

As a younger man I'd never bend with the fight.
I'd stand my ground whenever I thought I was right.

I would say to the tester who gave me the test,
"Give me your worst and then I will give you my best."

I faced the world with a will to right all wrong.
There were the growing days when my body was strong.

Whether at work or at play I needed no rest!
The more fate asked of me, the greater my zest.

Now that I am seasoned and my days but few
I question the thrusts that I am able to chew.

My will may still be young, my spirit just as strong,
But the strength of my body, the strength of my arm?

My dreams are just as daring. I still challenge fate;
Often cast aside reason and don't hesitate.

For I know in my heart, however clear the stream.
What pain or hurt can cut so deep, as life's lost Dream?

All Ages

They say be kind to all children,
    but that's only partly true.
Should you not be kind to everyone,
    ages one to ninety-two?

Remember how each of us who has
    lived long spans of years,
Loves to be treated as children,
    to be given children's cheers.

So do all our little children, as they
    walk the self same way,
Love to be treated as grown ups
    In the games of life they play.

This is the moral of my story,
    its obvious results.
You treat all adults like children
    and all children as adults.

Φ Φ Φ

Bits of My Philosophy of this Life

Destiny

I cannot make the hot sun shine brighter.

I cannot make the size of load much lighter.

Whatever the gods have destined for me,

Then that is exactly what I will be!

Φ Φ Φ

Sorrow

If I said it once, I've said it twice,

What's as limpid as yesterday's ice?

The same with tragedy. Trite but true.

No one wants to hear what makes you blue.

Φ Φ Φ

Account

What do you do when the bubble bursts
  And the venom seeps from within?

What do you do when the bubble bursts
  And says now account for your sin?

For account you must and account you will
  'Fore the brightest light grows dim!

For account you must and account you will
  For naught can be hid from Him!

Φ Φ Φ

I Believe

Even those who do not believe,
      want to believe.
Even those who do not achieve
      want to achieve.
The worst of all losers, a
      winning picture paints.
The worst of all sinners
      always think they are saints.

Φ Φ Φ

Hope

Hope is both a sword and shield,
A will that will never yield
To blind acceptance of what fates wield.

It pierces thru' the pain of doubt
It says "*watch me!*" hear it shout
"*Am I not what living is all about?*"

Φ Φ Φ

Truths

These are truths that I have come to know
Light within exceeds a diamond's glow.

And of all the joys a man might feel
Of all the ways a hurt heart might heal.

Every life is more than need and caring
What matters most is breed and sharing.

Φ Φ Φ

Kick the Ball

When you're depressed, think of me
And watch the way I bend my knee.

So wave your arms and look about
This life's no place to sit and pout.

Just kick the ball with your big toe
Say "*Hi!*" to today and off you go!

3/90

Φ Φ Φ

Misled by Size

How little seems the pigeon to an
    eagle or a hawk,
But to the pigeon little is the wren
    or a garden lark.

All things as to size relate to the
    size of he who looks;
Mighty rivers and mountain streams or
    bubbling country brooks.

Don't judge by the subject's size, whether
    skin is light or dark.
Among dogs and men, the littlest can
    have loudest bark!

Φ Φ Φ

Patience

However wrought the day.

However sad the night.

Patience and you'll see,

Troubles take their flight.

Φ Φ Φ

A Hotel Guest

On my travels while at the Russel Hotel in London I watched an aging, tired clean-up lady go from room to room.

Char Lady

From room to room she pushed her cart,
Cleaned each room and she left a part,
Of writing paper and bathroom soap,
Coupled with a waning bit of hope.

Swept the floors, polished mirrors clean,
Each room revealing a new life scene.
In room one, were the gray-haired two,
Both their kindly faces would speak to you.

In room two gray-haired and very wise,
An elderly gent with lonely eyes.
She thought, had she seen him years before,
With a wife whose whim he did adore?

And room number three across the hall,
Was the busiest room of them all.
There were two young girls with flossy hair,
Each drinking of life without a care.

It was the last room to clean each day,
Leaving tell-tale signs of youth at play.
The room that seemed to sing the best,
Was where a young child had been its guest.

From dawn to dusk, changing every bed,
Each pillow puffed, few words were said.
Mechanically she went her way,
A victim of the spoils life can play.

5/25/87

Φ Φ Φ

Reaching High

While flying from Europe, a young man seated in front of me reached to remove his lugguage from above his seat.

Hidden Power

He took his luggage from the rack,
Strained as he arched his back.

He shoved my cart from the top.
I feared great harm should it drop.

I wanted to call out and say
"You cannot push things out that way!"

Silently, I cursed the man,
Then saw his arm and crippled hand.

Shame to judge him, before I knew
The man had done what he couldn't do!

Reached beyond his handicap
What unseen power did he tap?

Φ Φ Φ

Miracles of Life

Throughout the years many taught me wrong from right
And my teachers taught me to know rote by sight.

My beautiful mother taught me how to think.
How to head-on meet the waves and never sink.

Black men, white men, and yellow too, did their part,
Teaching me the tenets of a human heart.

Hidden sources, some long forgot, some never seen,
Taught me the value of each human being.

But all the many that made up my life,
My sister, my brother, my children, my wife.

From them I thought I had learned living best,
All answers to my prayers on this life's quest.

And then long after a half century spent.
I saw the purpose of what it all had meant.

For with the learning that seems to never end,
Continuing to come from both child and friend.

The miracle of life I held in my hand.
Four little granddaughters and one little man.

                              2/10/89
                              4:30 a.m.

                    Φ Φ Φ

Living

What is freedom? What does it mean?
Is it substance? Can it be seen?

How free is one to speak his mind,
Less thought or care for brotherkind?

Allow our child to never know
The lessons taught when we say no.

How free is one to set one's pace
And cast aside the human race?

For who is free of inner pain
The desires that active minds feign.

Life's paths riddled with cutting stones.
Old age replete with brittle bones.

Wise men ponder, ponder a lot,
What can it be, what is it not?

10/31/91
4:30 a.m.

Φ Φ Φ

All Life is Intertwined

If man could see and he was not blind,
He'd know all life is intertwined.

The beggar begging when 'ere we meet,
The cooks who cook the very food we eat.

Each life that is, the great and the small,
Affects the welfare of one and all.

The king high upon his throne of gold,
The gardener lowly bent and old.

The winner to whom success is sweet,
The loser experiencing defeat.

The high towers of men who rule,
In garrets of each wandering fool.

A fine thread transcends both time and place,
Each a member of the human race.

Each breathes the same air, feels the same sun,
Each closes his eyes when his time is done.

The size of plot of his final rest,
The same for the worst as for the best.

1986

Φ Φ Φ

Promises

Many are the promises,
 we make before the win.
Promises which after we do
 rationally rescind.

It's not that we don't mean them,
 when first made.
It's just that pomp and grandeur
 cause promises to fade.

Φ Φ Φ

Meaning

It's not always the words we speak,
 or what we fail to say.
It's the caring well within, that our
 deepest thoughts convey!

It's the <u>Need</u> that's always known,
Not the pressures often shown.

It's the roses, the deer, the family ties.
It's walking life's path where our true love lies.

10/13/91

Φ Φ Φ

A Bird in Hand

There is a true story that I have been told;
About a wise man, one hundred years old.

He knew all answers to questions asked;
Saw all men, but never judgment passed.

Then one foolish youth sought to trick the man;
To belie any answer, that was his plan.

"Very Wise Man," he said, *"Please speak to me true,
For this is a test and I'm judging you."*

*"In my hand, nestled as if in a bed,
there lies a bird. Is it alive or dead?"*

To his friends, the youth did say *"Watch and see,
That wise old fool he cannot better me.*

*"If he says dead, the bird will away fly;
If he says alive, squeezed bird will die."*

The old man sighed and then sighed again,
He looked at the boy and said *"Young Friend,"*

*"This answers the question you asked me,
It is as you will it, so it will be!"*

4/88

Φ Φ Φ

The Sun

Let's watch the sun that lights the fray,
And guides the traveler on his way.

That never fails to come with dawn,
That shows the salmon where to spawn;

That heats the chill of early day,
Warms waters for a child to play;

That never fails to show its face,
Even if the earth should be waste;

And yet with all its light and might,
To create day where there was night.

It cannot warm the heart of man,
Or count grains in a sea of sand.

It cannot give a man a soul.
It cannot curb growing old.

Φ Φ Φ

Sid Tucker

How tall a man stands
     comes from within,
A soul where the good
     outweighs the sin.

The wealth of a man
     is measured, no doubt
By the esteem with which
     he is held without.

To have lived such a life,
     soft spoken and true,
Is a beacon to follow,
     for me and for you.

9/13/91

Φ Φ Φ

186

When the British Star was denied the Tony because she was only considered an English Star

The True Tony

Things are not always as they should be
In tribulations, triumphs and tragedy.
Justice does not always rear its head,
Jealousies and envies take the fore instead.

If I had a Tony of my own to give
To the best that I have seen in all my years;
To a lady who can make the unreal live
With a voice that won our hearts, to her, *'three cheers!'*

And so in this world of "*let's pretend*,"
Will you come please play the game with me.
Accept my Tony and let it blend
With your undisputed victory.

Φ Φ Φ

Intimates

Comfort is a grand, grand thing
    of which we should ne'er lose sight,
But never fail to meet the need
    to tease and to excite.

As I have often heard it said,
    from those who study art in bed.
Bring to boudoir from time to time,
    adventure tinged exotic rhyme.

This is the secret I confide,
    "Don't ever cease to be a bride.
Delight the night with sweet surprise.
    It all starts with what meets the eyes."

Φ Φ Φ

The Road Ends

Nothing is forever, good things
    all slowly end.
Life's roads are always winding;
    they, bump, turn and bend.

There are shut downs, delays,
    and so many detours,
Still the roads continue while
    the waterfall roars,

All men must walk their way,
    take turns and think a bit;
Change course when roads end,
    climb the bumps and bends of it.

Men will reflect on the roads
    that they have passed,
Of all the lives that they have known,
    the loves that last.

In their reflections,
  they will surely always say,
How thankful they are that
  they traveled this way.

Sure the bumps were hard
  and some of the best fled by,
But the memories will linger
  until they die.

   7/92

  Φ Φ Φ

OVERFEED

Overfeed

Said the stomach to the lip,

Take this friendly little tip,

Fill me gently thru the day,

Overfeed me and you'll pay.

Φ Φ Φ

LESSONS OF LIFE

194

I Know

I have grabbed the reins, rode the wind,
Lived like a saint but tasted sin.

For perfection in a man will fall.
Imperfection bits live in us all.

With a sight, a sound, a turn of head;
Memories of what my mother said.

The softness touch of a new born babe.
Parry-thrust of a bayonet blade.

I know secrets hide in every bed.
That is where forgiveness tears are shed.

The saddened eyes of men at war.
The trite moaning of a dazzling whore.

The depression depths that reason jars.
The very will to win, to reach the stars.

I also know that most men are weak.
I know that countless days are very bleak.

I know that every man's life contains
The best of days and his many pains.

I have known the fears that come with fright.
I've seen men soar to their highest height.

Dreams of youth and simply growing old,
Just pour and stir in life's mixing bowl.

I know best that people do stand tall
The times when you need them most of all.

12/13/87

Φ Φ Φ

WAR

A Marine Reflects

OH! The Glory Days! OH! The Wonder Days!
　　OH! The days back then;
When I marched in unison with a group of
　　proud strong men.

Remembering the commands once barked,
The lives that we met; lives that we marked.

The top kick asking, *"Are you mice or men?*
Are you fighting cocks or a mother hen?"

Fighting the battles, wherever they led,
Prayers for the living, tears for the dead.

OH! The Glory Days! OH! The Wonder Days!
　　OH! The days back then;
When I marched in unison with a group of
　　proud strong men.

Φ Φ Φ

Before my enlistment I worked at Bendix Radio's Crystal Plant on the graveyard shirt from 12 p.m. to 8 a.m. It was the days of the Bataan March, the dark days.

On to Victory

From the battered beaches of Bataan
To the shotfull skies of Scotty's Land;
Wherever free men make their stand--
      It's on to victory.

From the sugar shelf of the grocery store
To the toothpaste tins on the druggist's floor;
And from behind every closed garage door-
      It's on to victory.

From the cities' lights which are not lit,
From the hearts of all who do their bit;
The cry springs forth, "*We shall not quit*
      Until there's victory."

Wherever free men gallantly
Hold up the yoke of liberty;
Both in the air and on the sea--
      It's on to victory.

From the watchers' watch as he gazes high,
From the men on ground and the men who fly;
Their only creed is '*To do or die*'--
      It's all for victory.

From the men who fight and the men who pray,
From the mother's heart as her son goes 'way;
In every voice you can hear them say--
    It's all for victory.

No price my son is too high to pay,
With God's Will won, we'll save the day;
So do your best as only you may--
    All for victory.

The days ahead may be darker still
And blacker yet as they no doubt will;
But we dare not stop nor rest until--
    We have victory.

             April 26, 1942

    Φ Φ Φ

I had visions of reducing my Corps experiences to verse but you know what happens to the best of intentions. The activity of a Marine's day didn't provide time to write verse.

We Arrived

"All recruits over to the sidewalk",
    came the first command,
"Over to the sidewalk or in the
    Pits of Hell you'll land.
Now listen to me knuckleheads,
    get this through your dome,
You had better stop your thinking
    the way did at home.
You're Marines or at least Marines
    you're going to be;
You think I'm kidding but you'll
    soon learn differently."

Down deep inside we heard and laughed,
    and then with a calm sneer,
We muttered all sorts of thoughts
    we knew he could never hear.
The old *'Top Kick'* just looked in vain
    and spoke with much disgust,
"If this ain't the lousiest bunch;
    I've never before seen such."
He raised his hat, shut his eyes,
    and quickly wiped his head;
Then once more he gazed at us
    and the words that that guy said.

"When I tell you to get moving,
        I don't want to see you go;
I want to see you already there---
        excuses we never know."
We jumped over with our gear and wrap
        for the tone of that brisk voice
Caused our eardrums to shutter shut
        and left us with no choice.
Not giving him chance to speak again,
        before the wall we froze;
And as the roll was being called,
        we kept our rigid pose.

"Into the truck you ninnies!"
        the sergeant yelled once more;
"You're too slow," he looked and said,
        "Boys, please don't get me sore."
How we did it, I'll never know,
        could it be done again;
For as we crammed between those walls,
        frames began to bend.
"Take a deep breath you yokels;
        squeeze tight, here comes another score"
In they came and in they came,
        covering every bit of floor.

We rode in sardine fashion from
      the town of Yamassee,
Packed so close together that
      I knew not which was me.
Over the ocean waters,
      past the marsh and swampy land--
Suddenly we saw ahead
      tons of Parris Island sand.
Then, like a bunch of toy balloons
      who taste a breath of air,
Inside we burst with pride,
      knowing that at last <u>We Were There</u>.

November, 1942

Φ Φ Φ

We Were There

The hour was three-twenty as we
    entered this strange Isle;
A decent night of sleep we had
    not known for quite a while.
The trip was long and drowsy and
    the train ungodly slow;
Stopping at each and every known port
    and ports you'd never know;
It would start again and stop again,
    then start as before;
And ride for twenty minutes and
    then stop to rest once more.

Yes, the boys were mighty tired
    and anxious to rest a bit;
But the 'Sarge' had different ideas
    and that's all there was to it.
We stood before him, worn and weary,
    a-resting on one foot;
As into separate platoons
    we watched our buddies put.
Then with that ordeal finally over,
    another 'Sarge', we saw,
Who soon made it known that
    his word was to be our law.

We were led into a building
      and stood before the clerk,
Who asked us our name and age
      and then would yell *"Next Jerk."*
Our names already taken,
      through an open door we strode;
"Pick yourself up a poncho,"
      was our sergeant's very next word.
A poncho - just what is that for?
      None of the boys there knew
But quick indeed we were to learn the
      things that it could do.

We grabbed the rubber cover from
      off the pile so high,
And then to our sergeant's cadence,
      off we seemed to fly.
I never saw a man before whose
      steps were quite so wide;
Why we had to take a dozen steps
      to his every other stride.
There we trudged along, half asleep,
      our arms loaded down
With blankets and all the such,
      we tried to hold our ground.

It was a funny sight indeed,
     to see the rookies run
With arms full and dripping wet
     from the heat of the bright sun.
The same as we started,
     we came to a sudden stop;
Some of us were given brooms
     while others were handed a mop.
"Inside and clean those barracks
     and be sure that I can see
My face in every window,
     or a sorry lot you'll be!"

Our day was far from over,
     we started to clean the place
And shine every window so that
     the *'Sarge'* could see his face.
The hour was late when he came back
     and we were standing by;
He then looked at every spot
     where a speck of dirt could lie.
"Do you call this clean, you dopesters?"
     were the very next words he said.
"Well, you'll scrub this damn place over
     before you go to bed."

At last we were all through
      and the place was sparkling clean;
The windows had more sparkle
      than any I'd ever seen.
We rinsed the mops, washed the rags,
      put them all away;
And oh, how our weary bodies
      longed to hit the hay.
And so with our first day over,
      we laid us down with dreams
Of all the fame and glory
      of the United States Marines.

November 1942

Φ Φ Φ

A Marine

As I sit and use my pen,
The rain is coming down again.
The boys are lying here in bed,
Reading books, I've already read.

In our hearts are thoughts of home,
Of streets and fields we used to roam,
And as we sit we seem to hear,
The voices of those we hold so dear.

But somehow with every thought,
The things we have just been taught -
(To march, to fight, to shot, to drill,
How to live and how to kill)
Overwhelms every other thing,
As a sense of pride seems to sing,
"I'm a United States Marine."

To Gloria
11/30/42

Φ Φ Φ

Lest We Forget

Lest we forget in days of war,
The better days of peace;
Lest we forget with every chore,
The blessings that never cease;
Lest we forget each tottered mile,
The inspiration of a mother's smile;
Let's halt our passing now and then,
To think of these things once again.

Even though we may be far apart,
From those we hold so dear;
Their presence clings to our very heart,
As though they were so near.

The laughter that we used to know;
The places where we used to go;
Yes, let us halt and drink a toast
To those at home whom we love most.

> To my "*Home and
> Loved Ones*"
> December, 1942

Φ Φ Φ

Why We Fight

To live in peace, to rise each day,
To gaze upon our kids at play,
To watch those nimble feet of youth,
Go forth to learn the love of truth.

To know that should we disagree,
With those in high authority,
We may, with voices far from meek,
Shout forth the thoughts we care to speak.

To know that we may bow with grace,
Regardless of creed, sect, or race,
And pray to God how 'ere we choose,
A precious right we'll never lose.

This, my God is why we fight,
Guide us forth to win your right!

February, 1943

Φ Φ Φ

The commandant of my squadron together with thirteen crewmen died when flash bombs exploded in the Liberator B4 plane while returning to base. It was my plane. I had allowed a friend to take my place so that he could attend a family function. He was one of the thirteen. I wrote this editorial in the squadron paper.

There is little we can say and little we can do in memorial to those of our group who have left for the great beyond. Words are such futile things when standing before the subject of life --- words can never express the inner feelings of those of us who look upon the events of the past few days as <u>something very difficult to believe</u>. You and I knew them all. Many of us speak of the hours preceding the trip. We view with greater depth than we are apt to show, the realization that such is the price of war.

Ironically enough, it sometimes takes a tragedy such as this to stamp out the frivolity of the moment and to impress upon us the full weight of the task we have to perform. All else seems so petty beside death; or to think that<u> for any reason,</u> any one of us holds a grudge against any other one of the men with whom we are to live and fight! It is a mighty disgusting memory that brings to mind the words of old salts who sport with the fact that some of our number came from Selective Service --- they do not seem to realize that no initial prefix to a serial number or to a name offers any greater immunity from the scars of war.

To a world at war this is but a drop in a valiant bucket of blood. But to every mother <u>this is a son</u>; to every wife <u>this is a husband</u>; and to every child, <u>this means a life without a father</u>. These are not pleasant thoughts but no part of war is pleasant.

Do you remember the afternoon the Col. Pollock called us all together in the synthetic building and introduced both himself and the purpose of VMD -- 354 to us? Do you remember how he never ceased stressing the fact that he wanted to mold us into a working team *'second to none?'* Do you remember how he spoke of us as *'the gang'* and how he pleaded that each of us realize the seriousness of the smallest task we are asked to perform? And to you remember how he told us of the funny feeling he always got when he looked at the <u>vacant spaces</u> in the ranks of the gangs who returned?

It is now our turn to plead and to promise. WE'VE GOT WHAT IT TAKES AND MORE BESIDES! We <u>can be</u> a working team *'second to none'*! We can and we must realize the seriousness of it all and because of this realization, we must do our best *'however small the tasks may seem to be.'*

Let every conscience know (as we continue to taste the experiences of war) that it was not neglect or carelessness that boosted the number of these inevitable '<u>vacant spaces</u>!'

5/44

Φ Φ Φ

War

Part I

As any fool can plainly see,
War is always meant to be,
Killing is a cherished way of life.

Teach the young to go to war,
That's what youth is really for,
Killing is a cherished way of life.

Twist the blade, parry to thrust,
For indeed '*In God We Trust*,'
Killing is a cherished way of life.

It's the war to end all war!
Where have I heard that before?
Killing is a cherished way of life.

Part II

They were our hated foe,
Spreading death where e'er they'd go,
Is that enemy truly now our friend?

    Forget the lives our boys shed,
    The heart aches, the bodies bled,
    Is that enemy truly now our friend?

Indeed we had won the day,
Killed the fools, made them pay,
Is that enemy truly now our friend?

    Knock them down, then make them great,
    Pat their backs, they share our hate.
    Is that enemy truly now our friend?

Part III

What is meant by the '*Great War?*'
Counting coffins by the score?
Dare we cherish peace and say "*War No More?*"

    Stop war cries, stop the rally.
    Pros and Cons? Stop the tally.
    Dare we cherish peace and say "*War No More?*"

Should we prove history wrong?
Change our tune, change our song?
Dare we cherish peace and say "*War No More?*"

    Differences always exist.
    The sword solution we must resist.
    Dare we cherish peace and say "*War No More?*"

               In My Twilight Years

Φ Φ Φ

FRIENDSHIP

A Toast

Let's drink a toast, to the days to come,

To the familiar tunes we used to hum,

To the boys at home and the boys away,

Let's drink a toast as to God we pray.

Written to Siggie
11/27/42

Φ Φ Φ

To Paul

When most I needed a true friend,
You stood there, holding to the end,
And gave, not asking 'why' or 'when.'

These things, a man cannot forget,
These things, my friend, you'll not regret.

To Paul
1/11/43

Φ Φ Φ

Friendships

When we go home and tell this tale,

Nature's wonders on every trail,

Do not forget because it's true,

Of friendships made twixt me and you.

10/85
Africa

Φ Φ Φ

Good Folks

Others remember shipboard romances,

As for me, I'll always take my chances,

With good folks who dine where few many enter,

'Midst Lords and Commons they be the center.

To Chris Spivey
10/1/86

Φ Φ Φ

Ginny

It's time for reflection
    It's a time to decide
That time waits for no man
    There is no place to hide.

So let's save our pennies
    Each quarter and each dime
And travel together
    Like our "*Kenya Trip*" time.

            3/90
            Safari Souls

Φ Φ Φ

A Friend

Few values in life
    are quite so rare
As a friend who shows
    the will to care.
Who gives his heart
    and asks no return
Who uplifts and knows
    each thought you've sown.
When such friends appear,
    now and again,
Treasure them, love them,
    and be their friend.
How wealthy I truly am
    to know '*you*' as one of them.

1986

Φ Φ Φ

OLD AGE

Not Me

I ask "*How can it be?*

When around us we see,

Years show on face and limb,

Not on me, but on him!"

Φ Φ Φ

The Will to Try

I watched him slowly walk the road,
    he had a cane in hand,
His gait was soft, his head hung low,
    he was an old, old man.

His shoulders bent with time and age,
    his walk a chore indeed,
But go he must, so go he did,
    to go, it was his need.

He made me think of years gone by,
    my will so strong, my gait so spry.
He made me think of years ahead,
    pray I too have the will to try.

1985

Φ Φ Φ

Reflections

Look at me. Look at me.
    In the glass, what do I see?

What do I see in winters' chill.
    Gray hair, but eyes that sparkle still.

And through it all the waters flow.
    It's a new infant, the reflections show.

What do I see when I look
    At reflections in a flowing brook?

First an infant held in hand
    Then the first steps of a little man.

What do I see the next time 'round?
    A running child whose steps abound.

The waters seem to know no changes,
    Until our features it re-arranges.

What do I see this autumn day?
    A father with his child at play.

1989

Φ Φ Φ

Yester Year

Now that the remaining years grow thin,
    There are times I wonder where I've been.

With a touch of tear and bounds of joy,
    I think of days when I was a boy.

Think of them now as I thought of them then.
    Will I ever know those days again?

The children's prayer I said each night,
    The only prayer I could recite.

And now that I'm at three score and ten,
    I bow my head and say it again.

Φ Φ Φ

Dare I?

It's the doubts that seem to ever creep,
Into my daydreams, into my sleep.
How much quicker it is now to weep?
It's the pace I can no longer keep.

True that my gait has slowed a bit.
True that my mind seems to still be fit.
True! I cannot run the runner's mile;
But no matter the pain, life's worthwhile!

What I was I can no longer be.
Time has tolled the very best from me.
Albeit when the push comes down to shove
It's the thrill of the fight I still love.

Dare I pine and sleep my life away?
Dare I try to hide from light of day?
Dare I cease being a moving force?
Dare I, or do I yet have the choice?

12/92

Φ Φ Φ

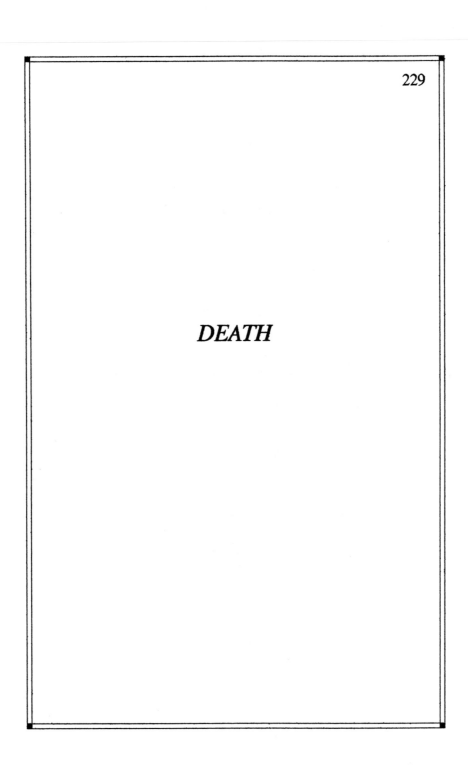

DEATH

Holocaust

How can a man alive deny?

Terror in a child's cry,

Watching its mother die,

Without a grave in which to lie.

Φ Φ Φ

Life's Passing

I cannot stop its flight.

I cannot stay its pain.

Life's passing is a must.

Life's memories its refrain.

Φ Φ Φ

The Inevitable

When I was young and bold and virile,
     I'd stand my own and never flinch,
I'd face the odds whatever they'd be,
     and never give an inch.

I would walk beneath the starlit skies
     as an Admiral of the sea.
Living in tomorrow's land and being
     whatever I chose to be.

Now that I am in the twilight years of life,
     past three score years and ten.
Those same visions of my early youth are
     the dreams that I dream again.

But time will take its toll in all we do,
     both men and their dreams grow old,
And all the marks we made, be they bad or good,
     live past the tales we told.

Moments lost are forever lost.
     What has been done cannot be re-done.
Make the most of the time allotted;
     give your best and the day is won.

For life is a course on the road to death,
     its days are the seeds we sow.
Knowing in heart, what all men know,
     wanting to stay, not wanting to go.

To our youthful eyes time is never ending,
     the years seem here to stay.
More seasoned years age with knowing that
     it's the piper we must pay.

Φ Φ Φ

To a young cousin who was given six months to live. How he accepted his fate was in my eyes a revelation.

After being with you and Marge yesterday evening and after reviewing the highlights of the Montaigne essay, of this I am certain, either Montaigne wrote of your philosophy of life or you wrote the essay and Montaigne got the credit for it.

There are those things in life over which we have no control. We accept them; we meet them and move about them as best we can; but the destiny decreed to each of us though often harsh and not understood is our only destiny and is our lot.

So many portions of Montaigne's description of how blessed man is to live life to its fullest, describes the togetherness that you and Marge have known. I tell you without any equivocation that I pray that I have the strength of understanding that you now show and that my children have the same, for the destiny decreed is not yours alone but will in time come to each of us.

You are loved by all who know you. I am proud to know that you are part of me.

Let God and his wisdom continue to give you the peace of mind and all the freedom from pain that a good man should know.

11/6/86

Φ Φ Φ

The principal of my high school who did so much to make certain I completed high school.

To '*Doc*' Edwards

It was another time--
    it was another life--
Tall, stately, understanding
    '*Doc*' Edwards--

Pre-War he changed
    class schedules
so that I could stay in school
    While working--

Post-War he gave me a
    City College diploma,
accepting U.S.M.C.
    Correspondence School credits--

How can I not remember?

Sleep well, gentle giant--

Φ Φ Φ

Mr. President

We walk this way but once.
There is a time to be born.
There is a time to die.
There is a time for laughter.
There is a time for tears.
We walk this way but once.

It is today in which we live.

It is with today that we must discover the warmth of Brotherhood; the blessing of serving our fellow men; the peace of mind that is known to the little man who humbly helps to ease the burden of his fellow man.

All in life is not joy, and so it is meant to be. Who can cherish peace more tenderly than he who has known the horror of war?

Who can love freedom with greater passion than he who has known the shackles of bondage?

Hunger is the best teacher of the joys of feasting, just as the knowledge of true sorrow enables man to best appreciate moments of happiness.

He has walked this way but once.
He has known the sorrows of life and the blessings of life.
He is no more.

His passing will not be forgotten.
However we differed in the days past, however we disagreed, our hearts are heavier with his passing.
He is no more.

God bless you Mr. President.

John F. Kennedy - Epitaph
"Walk This Way But Once"
11/22/63

Φ Φ Φ

Father and Child

"Remember me and always know
from whence you come or where you go.

I go with thee both night and day
I go with thee as you walk your way."

So said a father to his child
as the road soon came to its end.

"Remember all the bliss we knew
memories guide you round each bend."

2/90

Φ Φ Φ

A letter to a friend on the death of his wife

The source of life that dictates our fates rarely asks us our wishes or seeks our approval of the give and take of life- We live, we love and we long for the moments of yesteryear- but with it all memories induce laughter that breaks through the flow of tears. For all that went before never truly passes- the fullness of the years you knew was something I often saw and always admired. You were indeed blessed.

Φ Φ Φ

Grave Side

Shovel by shovel, they dig the grave,
Talking of food and when will it rain.
Covering the earth mound with grass cloth.
A resting place, free of fears or pain.

Soft, silent sorrow, prayers are said.
Few words spoken amid eyes wet with tears.
Some nod their heads when Rabbi talks
Only of good. Do I sense some leers?

3/92

Φ Φ Φ

To Rest

The mourners stand around me.

The heavens weep above.

To rest I lay my lady.

To rest I lay my love.

                    10/89

              At Al Grinspoon's
              mother's service

        Φ Φ Φ

TIn 1932 my father died, age 38. I was the oldest of three children, the youngest age one; I was age nine.

My Father's Time

I knew so very little of him,
    and yet I knew him well.
So little time to love him,
    remembering tales he'd tell.

How different things might have been
    if only he was there!
Would I have been a better man,
    my cupboard been less bare?

Had he always stood here to watch and
    show me how to grow,
What missed opportunities would have
    been mine to know?

If his advice I'd follow what would I
    have heard him say?
Would I have seen college? Would I
    have been allowed to play?

The fates that hover over us
    and mark our destiny,
Are fickle with decisions as they
    chart the life to be.

And if you could request to change
    a single way of strife,
Would all else about you be changed
    to another life?

Fates won't change an iota or
    different make their call.
The entire road once chartered is
    for us one and all.

No part of life would I change
    or different want to be.
I cannot help but wonder, with him,
    what changes would I see?

And yet all that I have spoken
    is me, and me, and me!
Nowhere have I questioned what
    living would let him see.

For indeed as the years have shown,
    the flowers from his tree,
Have blossomed bright and wholesome,
    how proud my dad would be!

1992

Φ Φ Φ

OTHER WRITINGS

Thoughts

If I am able to capture the thousand and one thoughts that dance through my mind as I write, and if I am also able to pen them as illustratively as they appear before me, I will compose either a piece befitting a master or a piece befitting a fool. These are my thoughts, uncensored, unabridged.

I am indeed a fortunate man, not because of material riches, but because of the inseparable closeness that lives in my home. My wife and my little boy are two blessings for which I am ever grateful. No man has greater wealth than the wealth of a healthy, mischievous, lovable son. The worries and the fears that preceded the birth of my child were but a small part of my trials as a parent. I often have pessimistic thoughts, particularly in moments of despondency and there were many moments before his birth when things went far from right. There was the agony of thinking that perhaps the unborn would be less than a normal, healthy baby. I was possessed with the wildest of thoughts and I did not dare mention them to anyone.

As a young man my mind often and perhaps unnecessarily tortured me. I was an imaginative youth and many of the figures of my imagination were black. Basically, I have never been an evil man, but my thoughts have often been evil thoughts. St. Augustine thanked God that he, himself, was not responsible for his actions in his dreams. This may be true, but surely the responsibility of the dreams you dream when you are awake cannot wholly be avoided. I am amazed at the memory of many of my immature thoughts.

Ever since I can remember, my home has been a place of shared emotion. The members of my family invariably showed their feelings for one another. Upon the lives of those close to me, I placed immeasurable value, but yet, I did not know the value of human life. I asked myself, "*what purpose does a man serve?*" I gradually matured. Age taught me the value of life. Experience seasoned the price of these values. I slowly grew to know that a man, the least of men, was in himself a priceless being. Experience is a wonderful teacher. No matter how still you stand, with the passing of time, you become inwardly richer in understanding. My years have shown me that the combined capacities of any one man, with that of any other man, is greater than the simple sum of the two.

The act of hate toward man plays no part in my philosophy, that is, hate as it is known to me. I interpret hatred as a feeling strong enough to desire destroying the object of the hate; and although there are many objects which I would willingly destroy, a breath taking being is not among them. I hate insincerity. I hate ignorance. I hate misery, poverty and want. I hate segregation. I hate inequality. The inequality to which I refer is the inequality of opportunity that comes as the result of the qualities in men of all the objects of my hate. Insincere men, ignorant men, men whose prejudices are amplified from poverty, misery and want, these are the men whose biased judgments refuse to allow them to deal with individuals as equals. These are the men who use as a basis for judgment "*is he white or black,*" "*is he Jew or Catholic.*" This is the same vile inequality that is bred in the social meetings of a village store and spreads to the selection of applicants for the colleges and for the professions. The inequality that knows no station but is in equal amount found among the learned and the illiterate. It is a terrible force often in the bosom of men who themselves are ignorant of its meaning or of its source. I am certain that the society foreseen by the founders of our country was a society free of this inequality.

As a child I took God to mean goodness. In the little actions of my little life, I interpreted God's goodness daily. If I were bad and if I stubbed a toe, I would say, *"God has punished me for being bad."* I knew God as a superior form of being. He was not to be questioned. My mind as a child accepted all the neither possessed the capacity nor the desire to siphon or to reject.

Maturity brought forth a natural development of mind. Books came into my life and with each work I read I discovered myself picking up a bit of philosophy that I interpreted as my own. My philosophies changed as my experiences varied. I discovered sex. From this association I gathered both in myself and in others my deepest understanding of the motives of men. My intercourse with living men and with the works of men long deceased prompted questions and changes of interpretation.

The God of my youth is the same God of my maturity. I have changed. He is constant. I think of Him as an unexplainable Force that is capable of molding and creating as only the God of the Bible or the God of nature can mold and create. My God lives not in the homes of the well-to-do, or in the magnificence of a church, or necessarily beneath the well dressed who attend church, but He lives within the hearts of good men. Wherever men breathe good, my God stands strongest, often in places of ill-fame and in the shabbiest of the most man-forsaken surroundings.

Φ Φ Φ

MY YEARS IN OPTIMIST INTERNATIONAL

Sharing

The best things in life are those which men must share
with others. How foolish I would feel to stand in a corner
and laugh to myself, for laughter and a smile have value only
when you share it with another. Is this not true of love?
What can more deeply affect the happiness of a man than the
sharing of love with a child or with a woman? Love, in
itself, has no value unless it is shared. How empty the life of
a teacher would be had he no child to teach. How empty the
life of an Optimist must be if he refuses to experience the
sharing of Optimism.

Φ Φ Φ

Community Service

"As I sow, so shall I reap" said the Optimist as he walked through the fields, dipping his right hand into his sack of grain and scattering the seed about the path of life he chose to walk.

The seasons pass. Amid the rays of sun and rains of heaven, life blooms from the seed as the grains of harvest grow.

Into the land has gone more than a scattering of seed. The OPTIMIST knows, better than most men, that it is not by chance that the harvest came but that it is by the sweat of brow and the preparation of mind to receive the fruits of man's labor.

Th OPTIMIST knows, better than most men, that all that is worthwhile in life often comes after many trials and many failures. There is no easy way.

This is COMMUNITY SERVICE.

This is OPTIMISM in its every purpose.

All that we do in OPTIMISM we do under the realm of COMMUNITY SERVICE. For we are the community and service to the community is service to our sons and daughters and service to ourselves.

What wonders are available to those of us who will partake. Man who has cultivated ideas, ideologies, technological growth, growth in all of the sciences, has left for his children yet unknown and untold wonders of the making of the better life. Words such as I write are not written to convey that which is theory but are placed before you, Mr. President, to convey that which is real; that which is today; that which is yours in your every approach to the men about you and to the life about you. What excitement you can impart and what satisfaction you can absorb in the planting of the seeds of a proper...

COMMUNITY SERVICE

The seed that you plant need not be of an original origin. It can be a seed that has been placed in your hands by others who passed before you. There is no monopoly in that which is good and he who presents that which is good, presents it for you and others like you to take and to develop---"*To sow that ye may reap.*"

Our community cries for men and women to take into their hands the INDIVIDUAL PROBLEM of the individual boy. The Boy who has a mind capable of development is often the boy who most needs the strength of direction that only a man can give a boy. Let us take the school drop-out and carry him back to the desperately needed development of education that awaits him in every community in this great land. This cannot be done by the best of written words, or by the finest of intentions, or by the most liberal spending of dollars. This can only be done on the basis of a man for a boy. Let this man for a boy wipe away from the young eyes the tears that show...and the tears that often fail to show. Let this man for a boy sole the worn shoes and replace the pants that may be too torn and tattered and listen with understanding to the expressions of fears of a young and growing mind. What wonders can we reap with a proper development of the school drop-out program? And what of this harvest? Our children will best see the fruits of this labor; for all things in this world are relative. The result of a man for a boy in the lifting up of the boy in whatever walk of life he may live, is the lifting up of our own son and the placing of our son in a better and more vibrant community. A man for a boy and the problem that has not been solved is solvable. This is COMMUNITY SERVICE.

ΦΦΦ

Grade Yourself

It is healthy and proper for each of us, as we travel through life, to occasionally stop and grade ourselves. This time for reflection is an opportunity to honestly appraise where we have gone and where we are yet to go.

Each individual should be graded in relationship to that same individual's ability to perform. It is in this manner that I ask each and every one of you to grade yourself.

Grade yourself with a (1), (2) or (3). Let (1) indicate that you have done all that you are mentally and physically capable of doing. Let (2) indicate that you have given a reasonable portion of your time and development in the furtherance of this wonderful philosophy of ours. Let (3) indicate that you have performed only to the extent of the necessity of performance, that you have done what you have had to do and volunteered little more.

All men are not equally endowed with the capacity to serve. Some give more of themselves than others only because they are capable of greater service. Others give less of themselves not because of a lack of capacity to serve but because of a lack of interest for service. It is the degree of service in proportion to the individual's capacity to serve that

<u>indicates true accomplishment</u>. Grade yourself not in relationship to what others have done but in relationship to the extent to which you have utilized your God given capacity for service.

It is with this measurement of self that I personally feel so lacking, for I know that regardless of the extent to which I have attempted to serve this year, my capacity is greater than that which I have utilized to date.

ΦΦΦ

Open the Door

Of all the fascinating experiences of this past year, the experience that has become a revelation is the discovery of the wealth of talent that lies within the breast of all the men about us.

OPEN THE DOOR to this talent, Mr. President. OPEN THE DOOR to this talent, future Governors. OPEN THE DOOR and the growth of this district will set an example for Optimism throughout the entire country. Do this and you will add richness and meaning to the lives of many men who eagerly await an opportunity to exercise many dormant talents.

How better can you serve your fellow men, Mr. President, than by OPENING THE DOOR. A minority of men in life are so fortunate as to discover that place in society which fits them best. Happiness in the work we do and in the life we lead is one of God's greatest blessings. Many a farmer dreams of his ability to be another Glenn and encircle the globe. Many a banker dreams of the land that he would love to till and the vegetation he would love to grow. Many a laborer dreams of the philosophy that he would love to propound for the generations yet to come. Each of us dream and each of us on occasion visualizes our performance in a change of our position in society.

The pangs of hunger in the hearts and minds of men for the development of their ability to deal with other men is ever present.

If you, Mr. President, awake in but one man among your

midst (not excluding yourself) the talent to perform, to create, to lead, and to serve, your year will have been a success.

If you, Mr. President, must personally and with exhaustion do all of the things that are necessary to complete a successful year without discovering the ability to inspire performance of the men about you, your year will have been lacking.

The key to all you are yet to do rests with the men with whom you break bread. Cut through the reserves, the introverts, the indifferent; cut through to the core that is ever present and every ready to mold the foundation of service. THERE IS NO MAGIC FORMULA. You, yourself must develop the capacity to see in the slightest remarks the clues to that which the man wants to do. Give to the man the job he wants to do. Give to the man the job he wants and he will astound you with the depth of his ability to perform. Challenge the man with the vitality of the responsibilities you have thrust upon him and he will further astound you with his performance.

Be selfish, be selfish and preach this selfishness to all of the members of your club. Be selfish in the sense that the development of this ability in yourself, in your position as leader of a group can only affect your ability to perform that much better in all of the things of life that you may in the future undertake.

The opportunity that lies before you may not come again. Do with it what you may but whatever you do with it, the responsibility of the end result rests with you alone.

Φ Φ Φ

EXCEPTIONAL CHILD SPEECH

GOD IN HIS INFINITE WISDOM DID NOT CHOOSE TO MAKE ALL MEN EQUAL. THE FORESIGHT OF THE MEN OF THE AMERICAN REVOLUTION EMBODIED IN LAW THE EQUALITY OF THE RIGHTS OF ALL MEN. THE RIGHT OF THE FREEDOM OF CHOICE OF RELIGION AND FREEDOM OF SPEECH AR SO DEEPLY ENTRENCHED IN OUR HEARTS AND MINDS THAT MANY OF US CONFUSE THE EQUALITY OF FREEDOM WITH THE EQUALITY OF OPPORTUNITY. THE COUNTRY WHICH EMBARKS ON A PROGRAM TO DEVELOP EVERY PERSON TO HIS FULLEST CAPACITY REGARDLESS OF ECONOMIC, RACIAL, RELIGIOUS, OR POLITICAL AFFILIATION WILL SURELY PROVIDE THE

LEADERSHIP OF THE WORLD...

MY OPTIMISM TELLS ME THAT IF YOU DEVELOP A YOUTH TO THINK FOR HIMSELF, THE POINT IS SOON REACHED WHERE HE WILL LIMIT THE EXTENT TO WHICH HE WILL ALLOW HIS ACTIONS TO BE DICTATED. THE THINKING MIND FULLY DEVELOPED BECOMES THE TRULY PERCEPTIVE MIND AND IT WILL WORK FOR THE BEST OF MAN RATHER THAN THE BEAST IN MAN.

IT HAS BEEN SAID THAT MEN DESERVE THEIR POLITICAL LEADERS. THAT THE END PRODUCT OF THE MEN WHOM WE PERMIT TO GUIDE OUR DESTINY IS THE DIRECT RESULT OF THE COMPLACENCY ON OUR PART WITH THE POLITICS OF OUR TIME. THAT THIS COMPLACENCY NOT ONLY DANGEROUSLY AFFECTS OUR PRESENT DAY LIVING BUT IT AFFECTS AS WELL THE DESTINY

OF OUR CHILDREN. HOW ASHAMED SO MANY OF US SHOULD BE FOR ALLOWING INDIFFERENCE TO SET IN.

IF IT IS TRUE THAT MEN DESERVE THEIR POLITICAL LEADERS, IS IT <u>LESS</u> TRUE THAT THE PEOPLE OF THE WORLD DESERVE THE TERROR AND FEARS THAT ARE FELT AS A RESULT OF THE LEADERSHIP <u>WHICH THEY HAVE PERMITTED TO COME INTO BEING?</u> AS MEN AND AS COUNTRIES, OUR RESPONSIBILITY TOWARD THE MAKING OF A BETTER WORLD IS AS UNEQUAL AS ARE THE ABILITIES WHICH WE AS MEN POSSESS IN RELATIONSHIP, EACH TO EACH. THOSE OF US WHO HAVE BEEN BLESSED...WITH JUST A LITTLE BIT MORE OF THE MATERIAL NEEDS OF LIFE <u>HAVE ALSO BEEN GIVEN</u> A PROPORTIONATELY GREATER

263

DEGREE OF RESPONSIBILITY IN THE WORLD WE BUILD FOR OUR CHILDREN.

IN 1787, BENJAMIN RUSH WROTE <u>THAT MEN SHOULD NEVER CONFUSE THE AMERICAN REVOLUTIONARY WAR WITH THE AMERICAN REVOLUTION</u>. HE SAID THAT IT WAS TRUE THAT THE WAR WAS OVER BUT THAT THIS WAS FAR <u>FROM BEING THE CASE WITH THE AMERICAN REVOLUTION</u>. ON THE CONTRARY, ONLY THE FIRST ACT OF THE GREAT DRAMA WAS CLOSED. OUR COUNTRY IS AS RESPONSIBLE FOR THE STATE OF THE WORLD AS IS ANY OTHER GOVERNMENT. WE ARE THE REVOLUTIONISTS OF PERFECTION. OUR FOREFATHERS CAME TO A WILDERNESS AND WITH A DESIRE FOR FREEDOM <u>PITTED MUSKET AGAINST CANNON AND WON.</u> WE WON OUR

FREEDOM WITH FORCE, ALL OF THE BLESSINGS OF WHICH WE PARTAKE TODAY ARE THE PRODUCT OF THAT FIRST ACT OF THIS DRAMA. AND YET <u>TIME HAS CLOUDED THIS VISION OF HOPE</u>. WE SOON LOST TRACK OF OUR RESPONSIBILITY TO ALL MEN. <u>OUR CAUSE WAS NEVER MORE VIBRANT THAN IT IS TODAY</u>. THESE ARE TRULY THE TIMES THAT TRY MENS' SOULS.

THERE CAN BE NO COMPROMISE WITH RIGHT. <u>COMPROMISE IN ITS PLACE</u> IS THE BLESSING OF DIPLOMACY AND THE NECESSITY OF POLITICS, BUT JUST AS I CANNOT COMPROMISE WITH YOUR LIBERTIES OR WITH YOUR FREEDOMS, SO CAN I NOT COMPROMISE WITH THE LIBERTIES AND FREEDOMS OF THE DOWN-TRODDEN PEOPLE OF THIS SMALL, SMALL WORLD. <u>THE BLACK GIANT</u>

WHO LIVES IN THE JUNGLES OF AFRICA HAS THE
SAME DESIRES AND THE SAME LOVES FOR HIS SON
AS I HAVE FOR MY SON.

THE WORLD WAS NEVER IN GREATER NEED OF
THE IDEALS OF FREEDOM, LIBERTY AND
EQUALITY THAT EXIST WITH SO MANY OF US NOW
AS COMPLACENT FACT. WE HAVE FAILED TO
RECOGNIZE THE FIRES OF FREEDOM IN AREA
AFTER AREA WHERE THE SPARK OF LIBERTY HAS
BEEN FOUND. WE STAND BACK IN HORROR WHEN
WE HEAR OF GUERRILLA BANDS IN FAR AWAY
LANDS WHO HAVE ATTACKED WITH FORCE THE
DECAY OF THEIR SYSTEM OF GOVERNMENT. WE
FORGET SO EASILY THE MEN OF THIS LAND WHO
STOOD BEHIND TREE STUMP AND BOULDER AND
WHO FIRED INTO THE MARCHING COATS OF RED,

RED, TEARING RED BREAST AFTER RED BREAST IN ORDER THAT OUR CRY OF FREEDOM BE ALLOWED TO LIVE. IT IS SO EASY TO FORGET AND SO NECESSARY TO REMEMBER. WHEREVER PROGRESS HAS BEEN MADE IN THE LIVES OF MEN, IT HAS BEEN MADE BY A MINORITY, BY MEN WHO DARED TO BE DIFFERENT.

THE WORLD NEEDS SCIENTIFIC ACHIEVEMENT AND ACADEMIC ACHIEVEMENT, BUT IT ALSO NEEDS <u>TO A FAR GREATER DEGREE</u> THE DEVELOPMENT IN MEN OF THE ABILITY TO DEAL WITH MEN.

IN AN AGE WHEN CONTINENTS BECOME NEIGHBORS AND WHERE THOUSANDS OF MILES OF DISTANCE BECOMES BUT HOURS IN TIME OF TRAVEL, THE HOUSE THAT BURNS IN THE MOST

REMOTE PART OF THE GLOVE IS A FIRE IN THE HOME OF A NEIGHBOR AND WE ARE AS DUTY BOUND TO CONSIDER AND TO HELP IN THE EXTINGUISHMENT OF THE FLAME AS WE WOULD BE IF THE FIRE BURNED IN THE YARD ADJOINING THE PLAY PENS AND THE SAND PILES OF OUR CHILDREN IN OUR OWN BACKYARDS.

AND SO IT IS WITH THE CRIES FOR FREEDOM AND FOR A BETTER LIFE THAT BURNS IN THE HEARTS OF MEN AND WOMEN IN THE MOST REMOTE PARTS OF THE GLOBE...

A RICH RELATIVE IS A RICH RELATIVE NO MATTER HOW GOOD HE ATTEMPTS TO BE TO HIS LESS FORTUNATE KIN. WHATEVER HE GIVES, HE CAN NEVER GIVE ENOUGH. IT IS IMPOSSIBLE TO SATISFY THE APPETITE OF MEN BY MATERIAL

THINGS ALONE. HOW MANY TOYS HAVE WE GIVEN OUR CHILDREN ONLY TO FIND <u>THAT IT IS THE ITEM THEY DO NOT HAVE</u> THAT THEY WANT THE MOST. YOUTH WANTS EVERYTHING. THEY WANT TO TASTE EVERY EXPERIMENT. THEY WANT TO EXPERIENCE <u>EVERY EMOTION</u>.

MONEY AND MATERIAL WEALTH ALONE WILL NOT SUFFICE IN WINNING THE PEACE OF THIS WORLD. <u>THEY ARE ESSENTIAL ELEMENTS</u> BUT THEY ARE <u>BUT A PART</u> OF A FAR GREATER NEED. THE UNDEVELOPED COUNTRIES OF THIS WORLD REQUIRE UNDERSTANDING AND COMPASSION <u>TO A FAR GREATER DEGREE</u> , THAN THEY ARE WILLING TO ACCEPT MATERIAL ADVANCEMENT. WE ARE IN DIRE NEED OF THE EXCEPTIONAL MIND. THE MIND IN WHICH THERE EXISTS THAT

LITTLE BIT OF SOMETHING THAT IN MOST INSTANCES DEFIES DEFINITION. IT MAY BE LIKENED <u>TO THE SPARK OF GOD IN CERTAIN BOYS AND MEN</u> THAT GIVES THEM THE SENSE OF FEELING, THE SENSE OF TOUCH, A POWER TO SEE THAT WHICH LIES BENEATH OR EXTENDS BEYOND.

WE SEE IT IN ALL WALKS OF LIFE, IN ALL OF THE PROFESSIONS, JUST AS WE SEE IT WHEREVER WE FIND LEADERSHIP. IN A CLASSROOM OF DOCTORS <u>ALL EQUALLY TRAINED</u>, ALL NOBLE AND SINCERE, EVER SO OFTEN, THERE CAN BE DISCOVERED THAT GOD-LIKE QUALITY THAT IS THE PRODUCT OF <u>NEITHER TEXTBOOK NOR TEACHING</u> -- BUT THAT LITTLE SOMETHING THAT MAKES THE ONE DOCTOR STAND ALOFT FROM THE OTHERS. THE SAME LITTLE SOMETHING THAT

ALLOWS THE LIGHT OF ONE MAN'S EYES AND HEART <u>TO PENETRATE</u> INTO THE EYES AND HEART OF HIS FELLOW MAN. CALL IT INSTINCT, CALL IT WHAT YOU WILL, BUT IT IS VITAL TO OUR LIFE AND TO THE LIVES OF OUR CHILDREN THAT WE DISCOVER THE POWER TO RECOGNIZE THIS QUALITY AND TO HELP THOSE WHO POSSESS IT TO DEVELOP IT AND TO USE IT FOR THE CAUSE OF GOOD -- TO USE IT TO HEAL RATHER THAN TO DESTROY.

THE HOPE OF THE WORLD LIES IN THE CONQUEST NOT OF OUTER SPACE BUT IN THE CONQUEST OF INNER SPACE. SOMEWHERE IN THE HIDDEN JUNGLES IN THE HEARTS OF NEWLY BORN COUNTRIES <u>AMONG THE MOST PRIMITIVE</u> AND

THE MOST NON-INSPIRING OF ATMOSPHERES, THERE MAY BE FOUND A LITTLE BLACK BOY WHO POSSESSES THE ABILITY TO DISCOVER A CURE FOR CANCER, OR THE YELLOW-FACED ARAB LAD WHO MAY HOLD IN HIS HEART THE SECRET OF PEACE.

IT IS HERE THAT THE MEANING AND THE PURPOSE OF OUR OPTIMISM COMES TRUE. YOU ARE THE LAMP LIGHTERS WHO DIRECTLY AND INDIRECTLY SEARCH OUT TO FIND THE BOY WHO HAS AN "ANSWERING LIGHT."

IT IS YOUR JOB TO LIGHT THE FIRES "FOR FROM A LITTLE SPARK MAY BURST A MIGHTY FLAME."

ΦΦΦ

Report to Convention at End of Year

And for those of you who have occasionally said we are too crowded in an area for new units, I tell you that you should see the men who have come into Optimism this year. In Cumberland when we sat down in the home of the Supervisor of Design of the Hercules Powder Company together with two of his assistants, a man who has one thousand men under his direct command, a man who perfected the solid fuel carrying missile items that sent our astronaut around the world. You heard this man talk and you left with a signed application. Optimism is the best product in the world to sell with some of the finest salesmen I have ever seen and we haven't even gotten started.

...Do you know that the Police Department of the City of Cumberland refused to give out a license on a bike, until that bike passed the Optimist of Cumberland inspection for fitness? They work in conjunction with teams that go from school area to school area, a member of the Police Department and members of the Cumberland Optimist; how many lives have been saved?...You and I will never know. We are all Optimists, but we must also be realistic. There is and there will always be in our midst, a percentage of men who continually require a little rejuvenation as far as Optimism is concerned...they have a tendency of asking why and telling you why it can't be done, with a lot more impetus than they take to tell you how it can be done. This is a normal course of affairs, it is something that we have experienced in the past. It is something that we will live with as long as we are on this earth. It serves many purposes. It prevents complacency on our part. Knowing the extreme of the Optimist thinking and the Pessimist thinking is as necessary to be a successful Optimist as it is to accomplishment in life. You must have comparisons. Differences. There have been differences. These differences existed in a very small segment of your District. These differences have come from qualified and very capable men. As adult men we should recognize one principle made in the Inaugural Address of one of the first Presidents of this country. He said..."*it takes a big man to realize that differences in program do not indicate differences in principle.*" Differences are welcome. We buy them, we need them. They have not taken away from our vitality and strength, they have added to it....I look around the room and it's a moment of memory. The first man I happen to see is Ward Heck. I'll never forget a night when Ward asked me to come to a regular meeting of Middle River, and I told Ward before and I have told him since, I didn't want to go to that meeting. I was tired. I had had a rough day. I was ready to pick up the phone a dozen times and say, "*Ward, please excuse me tonight.*" I went to that meeting and I thought I was at a convention. I saw 25 potential Optimists in that room together with 30 to 40 Middle River Optimists. The spirit in that room did more to relieve my tension than any tranquilizer could ever hope to do. We attempted to sell Optimism. Do you know the result?...sixteen gave in paid applications.

So much originated in the clubs. I hope and pray Optimist International reviews our sponsorship of Law Day U.S.A. in conjunction with the American Bar Association. Tim Helferstay who started the program on its way; the interest that I saw in men who had expressed no interest for many years.

My report is these memories, most of you know what has happened this year. Whatever man stands here next year, what a truly wonderful experience he has before him.

Hands Speech

God gave every man two hands, hands with which to write books, hands to pray, to hold a baby, to love a woman.

It was said that one hundred governors ran this district last year; and that is true. One hundred governors ran this district and I am the fortunate one to receive the ring which each of you deserve. I thank you for a year of memory that will never die. You have taught me that there is one thing about which we will never disagree ...and that's the right to disagree. We have differences. Some which we resolved, some which we will never resolve. It was a time for change. You helped open the door for all to serve without censor. You gave a man a job and you let him perform We disagreed occasionally, but all in all each of you accepted a job and went to and did what had to be done. I got a ring for it. I'll wear this ring so long as I have the good judgment and the good sense to realize it's no harm to stand alone, if what you stand for is that you feel is right. My heartfelt thanks to each and every one of you.

ΦΦΦ

*RESPECT
FOR THE LAW*

*Composed for a law client to express their
philosophy of the meaning of America*

Law Day 1966

What is it that makes this land of ours so great?

What is it that stirs the emotions of all free loving men, this LAW DAY U.S.A.?

What is it that warms the hearts of all Americans, regardless of their race, color, creed, or place of birth, this LAW DAY, U.S.A.?

Is it the freedom to seek our God in whatever House of Worship we might choose?

Or is it the freedom to choose to DISBELIEVE and not to worship Him at all?

Is it the vastness of these lands of ours, with our valleys, our waters, our mountains, and our plains?

Or is it the ground where the soil is rich and anxiously waiting to conceive, as compared to the ground where only stones will grow?

Is it the conformity of the principles of all Americans as to their rights of LIFE, LIBERTY AND THE PURSUIT OF HAPPINESS?

Or is it the wondrous non-conformity of free minds and of free thoughts and of the stepping stones that our forefathers have created from what might have been stumbling blocks?

Is it the stubborn aggressiveness of our forefathers in reaching plateau after plateau of fresh accomplishment in adding to the dignity of all men?

Or is it God's Grace in instilling in these adventurous men

their thinking that "*We do not want to know what we cannot do?*"

Is it the freedom to meet in fellowship and brotherhood with men of our own choosing, regardless of race, color or creed?

Or is it the freedom of choice not to so meet?

Is it the tape (often called red) that holds together the vastness of our governing bodies, be it on a local or a national level?

Or is it the dash and the spice of raw politics and the politicians who have the WONDERFUL audacity to cut the "*RED TAPE*" and often reduce to size the "*ALL IMPORTANT*" bureaucratic giant?

Is it perfection in our government structure and in our way of life?

Or is it the beauty of understanding hearts that know that perfection in men and women is in truth the proper proportion of imperfection?

Is it the zealously guarded right to vote for the party of your choice or to vote for the candidate of your choice regardless of party?

Or is it the choice not to exercise this rare and wonderful franchise?

What makes America great --- No simple one of these things. The greatness of this land is the proper proportion of all of these things --- the rights of men and the wrongs to men --- and the never ending struggle to do better. The bigots and the patriots, the black men and the white men, the law givers and the law takers --- America is all of those things.

But above all else, America is the fear of God that good men know and it is the relationship of that God to the wonders of this land, constantly promoting good men to be better men.

It is the right of each father to build for his son, and the pride of each father who watches his son far surpass the best of accomplishment that the father ever hoped to know.

It is this and it is more.

We Must Create a Worthy Example for Youth

A prosperous society is forever beset by mores of potential destruction. These internal, self-rationalized, accepted roots of decay are threats to society far more grave than are the threats of the military of nations or of the fanatical power-hungry men who lead such nations. We have heard this said in many ways. We have heard it from the pulpits. We have heard it in the schools -- but hearing it is not enough, for too many of us hear and fail to heed.

The youth about us are an advanced group. They are the product of a world in which communication from and exposure to the words of demagogue and devil are but everyday occurrences. My son has an awareness in his fifteen years of life which I did not have in my initial twenty-five years of life.

This is a very wonderful thing in that it permits the growth and development of young minds to degrees that we in our youth never conceived as possible. This is also a grave and serious matter in that the receptive minds of the young have before them all types of knowledge, and as the volume of knowledge increases, the screening and the lecturing on what is morally right and what is morally wrong becomes more and more difficult. Moral right is taught to children by men. Moral right is inbred, it is not inborn.

Each day we shatter the dreams and illusions of youth because of the quality of men in high places. The examples that we set soon become permanently imbedded in these developing minds. Headlines breed fear when one wonders how the young are able to separate or distinguish the good from the lawless. There is no explanation for the actions of many of the leaders of society who push all law and right aside when that right or that law interferes with monetary gain.

The headlines which read, "*Dairies Fined for Rigging Milk Prices*" represents tragedy. The insured losses of business against embezzlement and dishonesty have become as great, if not greater, than the insured losses of the same businesses against the uncontrollable force of fire. One can cite scandal after scandal.

There are the rigged TV quiz shows, scandals in high government places, conflict-of-interest cases in large and well regarded corporations, price fixing by industrial officials. The everyday payoff has become essential to many professions and many businesses. If you want a thing done, you must pay for it, and this does not mean the normal cost of payment but a showing of appreciation, the passing of dollars for expected service. The doctor who pays for the special hospital privilege destroys more than he builds. The Goldfines and the Adams are the givers and the takers. Group them all together and they spell out a complete disregard for moral right resulting in a self-implied immunity from the law of the land.

The taking of the easy way precedes the rationalization by the amateur of his right to take. How easy can this rationalization must be? The driver of the milk truck who pockets an extra dollar convinces himself that compared to the executives of the dairy who have pocketed extra thousands of dollars through their manipulation of prices charged for milk served to the school children of this community, he is a Saint. Try to offset this argument? It is not an easy task. I wonder who is more guilty, the giver or the taker. Goldfines cannot exist except for the Adams who are willing to take. Every traffic ticket that you fix, every special privilege that you buy, sears your moral fibre. There is neither room for rationalization nor can there be any compromise with what is morally right and what is morally wrong.

Our efforts can perhaps do little to alter the character of the men who now fall into the category of either giver or taker. We become set in our ways, we have assured ourselves that what we are doing is not morally wrong. We are convinced that these actions harm no one. We know that these words only apply to the other fellow.

The tragedy rests with the examples we set for the maturing mind of our youth. When we define what is right and what is wrong by so narrow a line, how can we expect our children with their tender years to know where they dare not step? How recklessly we trample on the young minds' ability to truly know the difference between what is moral wrong and what is moral right. *"Let he who is without sin cast the first stone"* and which of us dare toss a pebble?

The danger comes with the acceptances by *"we good people"* of the practices of which I speak. We are rarely alarmed about the embezzlement by the banker or the daily bribing of an employee (whether it be state, city or private enterprise) in order to do business with his employer. There is little concern with these practices. There is instead braggadocio by the men who practice it, both those who receive and those who give.

You and I accept it as a pattern and laugh when stories about it are told and occasionally think think the giver is a pretty shrewd fellow to have achieved what he has achieved. There is a danger when we accept these defects in society's moral fibre. There is a danger when we condone a pattern that has ruined greater societies in their day than perhaps we are in our day.

Let us take the magic of "*Law Day U.S.A.*" and develop it in our individual communities with all the wealth of our imagination. Let us create excitement in the adventure of what is right. Let us take to the youth the blessings of this land and show our sons the sentiment and thrill that each of us has experienced at some time in life upon hearing the Star Spangled Banner. Let us take this day but let us not take it lightly. If we are to create an image worthy of a child to follow, we must do it now for tomorrow may be too late.

5/1/63

Φ Φ Φ

LIFE AT
HAR SINAI
CONGREGATION

PRESIDENT'S MESSAGE

THE QUESTIONS

WHY belong to Har Sinai?

WHY devote time to enhance and insure the future vitality of Har Sinai?

WHY give dollars?

WHY participate in the life of the congregation?

WHO needs it?

THE ANSWERS

I need it! I need to know that the meaning of my faith perpetuates itself not only for my grandchildren but for your child and your grandchild. I must never forget that the way of life and my place in life is ever changing. I am no longer the robust youth of yesteryear, strong of arm, willing to stand up to any challenge and always able to hold my own.

I could not this day pass through the rigors of Paris Island Boot Camp being tested twenty hours per day, training that even then taxed my physical endurance. I must accept that the years that have passed have not only changed the physical me but they have changed so many of my life needs and wants and dreams.

I look back upon the passing years and see again those life events that passed beyond my ability to understand why. The death of a brother, the passing of parents, the periods of pain. The never ending deaths of the young men with whom I served, so alive one moment and forever gone the next. My reasoning furnished no answer to these life events. I did not understand the reasons then; I do not understand them now. I learned early on that where reason stopped, faith began. Without something in which to believe I would be lost. Tears alone are not relief enough from tragedy - I must have faith. I know that no matter how much material wealth I have there are those events beyond my ability to cope - I have needs. I have needed my Rabbi to name my child, I have needed my Rabbi to comfort me when all I saw was darkness. I have needed my Rabbi to bless my children, to teach my children a way of life that goes beyond material things. I will need my Rabbi to comfort my family, to mourn with my family when I pass my last day. I need the comfort of those friends I have grown to love in this congregation. Those friends who ask nothing material of me and never cease to show caring. I need to belong. I need to feel the magic of my people on Yom Kippur day. It is a time when I most realize that you and I are true examples of the impossible - we are part of a people whom anyone can rationalize should no longer exist - a people who have defied with only their faith tortuous acts of history which sought to destroy us. We are still here - the torturers have passed into oblivion. I need these things, but don't we all?

Sidney Kaplan

Φ Φ Φ

It's All About People

After half a century, one would think he or she had seen most of what Har Sinai is all about. Thru the years, its strength has been its adaptability to circumstances as they existed at specific points in time.

Its glorious history is second to none -- its free pulpit has espoused ideas far ahead of the times -- its movers and shakers have never failed to grasp the reins and lead.

But now I see a Har Sinai I never saw before -- it is one thing to sit in the sanctuary and watch the faces of those on the bema -- it's another thing to sit on the bema and watch the faces of all in the sanctuary -- and what are the differences one sees?

You first become cognizant of the people who truly breathe life into this house of life.

You see dozens of members who possess some mystic way of knowing what needs to be done -- and doing it before anyone has the time to ask. These are the true movers and shakers -- they give of themselves without reserve -- they don't seem to know the words "*No!*" or "*I can't!*" They are proof positive that Har Sinai will never die.

And so to all the wonderful people who make me proud of my Temple -- To all of you who share with me and my family the ties of being part of Har Sinai -- I wish you and yours God's greatest blessing, "*Peace of Mind*" and pray that your year ahead brings you health and happiness.

Sidney Kaplan
9/4/91

Φ Φ Φ

A New Year

A new year is about to be hatched. The chicken is the world about us. The egg is the substance of life for all people -- Arab and Jew -- Russian and American -- black and white -- semite and anti-semite. All people will partake of the egg -- breathing the same air -- seeing the same sky -- walking the same earth, same sun, same moon, same stars; and, in some respects, the same dreams, the same family ties.

So many similarities being shared -- birth, body parts, laughter, tears and death.

How is it that with so much the same, the differences which weigh so much less that the similarities tear apart the relationships of man?

Experience has shown that governments do not cause man to *'intertwine'* -- and is it not so that armies do not -- religion has not!

Is it because the failure to see by those few who refuse to *'intertwine'* stops the process for the many? If this is so, what hope does the future hold?

During World War II, at a night sports event in a packed Memorial Stadium, someone addressed the crowd. The purpose was to demonstrate the need to respect the blackout. The subject was how meaningful is the light from a single candle. Each of those present had been given a thin birthday candle upon entering the Stadium.

All lights went out. The night was pitch black. *"Now,"* said the speaker when it was too dark to one to see, *"Light your candle!"*

A single candle was lit, then another and another and another -- the black of night was soon enveloped in a sea of light -- everyone could see his brother! The glow was magic. Night became day.

And so it is, each of us who is an integral part of an institution such as Har Sinai -- the joining together of each of us -- the smile given to one who is without smiles and has so little to smile about -- the honest interest in the mitzvahs of Har Sinai life just waiting to be shared -- the giving of oneself to the blood drive or to help in a soup kitchen.

All of these things are a start -- the lighting of a first candle.

Is it possible that our reaching out to each other can become contagious not only within our House of God but in the greater House of God that touches all people of this city, this country, this world?

Perhaps not, but dare we fail to try?

Sidney Kaplan
10/30/91

Φ Φ Φ

Our Turn

Simchat Torah the house was overflowing with excited kids aged 1 to 71. It was indeed the largest attended non High Holy Day service I have experienced at Har Sinai.

The Torahs walked!
The Torahs talked!
The Torahs danced!

Little hands and lips reached out to kiss the Torahs, including the Torah that I carried.

Magic moments!
Exciting moments!

Little lips that could not reach the Torah in my arms until I leaned down to the eager hands and lips of the beautiful little people.

Then they danced and laughed and again and again touched the Torah. A beautiful and bountiful evening of rejoicing in a House of God.

Yes, it's now OUR TURN, not only to assure that such events continue to but assure their continued growth.

Tomorrow it will be THE TURN OF THE YOUNG FAMILIES of today to replace our financial support of today-down the years the little of the night just past will take THEIR TURN!

Sidney Kaplan
President

Φ Φ Φ

Joe Berney

He played many parts in this drama of life - to five grandchildren he was Pop Pop - to three children he was a father - to Jennie he was something special, a life companion, a safeguard against loneliness - he needed his Jennie.

He played the part of a safeguard, a guardian of trust of the welfare of Har Sinai - He was its treasurer - He was its spokesman - He lived hope when many lived despair - He was the optimist as to Har Sinai's undaunted growth -He loved your Har Sinai with a passion - so much of his life was intertwined with the life of the congregation.

But he was more!

He was your President - the President of the oldest continuous reform congregation in America - your congregation. Joe Berney loved every congregant, even those whom he only knew by name - He loved each child who was a part of Har Sinai culture - Joe cared. He was mystified by the fact that so many of the wonderful people who are part of Har Sinai have so little time to give to their faith and to their Har Sinai. Just last issue he spoke of his inability to understand the lack of time given to an institution that can return two fold so much of that often unobtainable greatest of God's blessings, *"Peace of Mind."*

Joe Berney knew this secret - He spoke of it - He told how every moment spent at Har Sinai House, at the chores of pleasures of Har Sinai's life, enriched his life and often made him stand ten feet tall.

Your Rabbi knew him well and told you much of the man - what the Rabbi's words may not have said but what his heart knew so well, was that Joe Berney stood as a father figure to many who touched his life and knew his heart.

But he was more!

He is part of the heritage of the best Har Sinai has to give.

Perhaps we would all grow in stature if we too let ourselves experience the Har Sinai heritage. Perhaps we too would experience the enrichment of soul that Joe Berney experienced. Perhaps, ever most important, our children and our children's children would experience in their precious young lives the same enrichment. The enrichment is there for our taking.

FROM MY LETTERS

Yesterday I felt differently than I have ever felt before concerning the war and the war's effects on all peace loving men. I never quite realized before just what hate is; I have always said that I hate no man. Perhaps hate and its meaning stood far away from me only because I had never taken time to think of the word. I must know hate. No man could feel the way I felt yesterday without knowing it.

'*Hate*', that is such an ugly word; thoughts of hate are such vile thoughts. When one feels hate, he is blind to all else. He can only see what has been done and because of what has been done, what must be done. '*Hate*' and '*War*', the two go hand in hand.

It is bitter for a man to stop and let all the hell out of the past few years pass before him in review. Just watching the parade is not enough; but when he sees the features of those he loves and holds so dear, substitute for the unfamiliar features of just another mortal, then and only then do these scenes of living hell have real meaning. Perhaps it is best to let the past rest in the past and to await the future with full confidence -- but, my dear, since my mind is such a strange mind, try as I may, I cannot blot out those miserable visions.

To see the pure wholesome bodies if my little sister, of my mother...mutilated by the savage lust if barbaric man, is more than I can stand. To see the word of my God and the works of my God abused by those same loathsome hands; to watch the old and the ill, all that I have been taught to respect, destroyed and maltreated by those same beasts; to see the honest tears of those sincere friends who feel the touch of the war as I do, spread films of fire across peaceful eyes; to see these things is more than I can stand.

My body and soul run away from me. I am no longer the average young man who yesterday longed for a career in law, who yesterday stated "*I hate no man*", who yesterday dreamed of love and its blessings, who yesterday walked unalarmed in a world of chaos, who yesterday said "*such things don't happen*," who yesterday walked well out of his way in order to avoid trouble, who yesterday watched the school children fill the playground as the school bell rang, who yesterday passed by the waving colors and merely looked aloft and said, "*Old Glory, may she wave forever.*"

Instead of being the peace loving boy of yesteryear, I grow to know hate, to want to kill, to be blind to all about me but the goal of the nearest Nazi throng and yet -- what do I hate? Can I say I truly hate the blonde German youth who was born of a mother just as I, who loves his mother just as I; that same youth who grew in his part of the world into his way of life just as I grew in my proud land into my way of life. On the Sunday that I rode through the cool green of the open country...could I have willingly taken the life of my blonde brother? Could I have torn apart the body and thrilled at the sight of his blood and without hesitation repeated my acts on his nearest kin? Could I have killed on that and thanked God for letting me kill, for giving me the strength and the will to kill? If I were in my blond brother's position and he were in mine, would he have not felt the same as I?

Yet today, such a short way ahead, I await the hour when my time to kill shall come; but that word hate, that vile word.

Yes, I now know hate, hate in its most bitter form. It is not the boy of that land whom I hate. It is not the son of that grey-headed suffering mother. He is a man just as I am a man. He lives and has a right to live, yet I must take that life or he will take mine---and yet, I know hate. No, my hate is not a hate of man, for my God has said all men shall love each other. My hate grows strong and my heart hardens, not for the boy, but for the cloth upon his back, for the things for which the emblem on his arm stand.

I hate *'hate'*, I love *'life'*; but to destroy this hate and to free this life, I must first destroy the boy I knew in yesteryear.

In place of the peaceful youth steps forth a soldier--an American fighting man whose temper is hot, whose wit is sure, whose might stands ready--A fighter in whose mind there can be no place for thoughts of a career, nor for doubts, nor for overconfidence in either his country or himself--A fighter who realizes that unless his mind is clear, unless he thinks quickly and reacts even more quickly, he will not suffice--A fighter who knows that such things can and have happened, and that it is entirely up to him and others like him to keep such things from happening again.

A fighter who knows that it is useless to walk out of his way to avoid trouble, especially these troubles that affect the world and all its occupants--A fighter who now knows that the only way to beat such trouble is to face it straight and sure, and to be able to return just enough more trouble than his opponent can take.

A fighter who although he no longer has the peace of mind with which to dream of life, of love, and of a career, knows only too well that these things depend solely on the outcome of the fight he now wages.

A fighter who now looks aloft at the banner that God has blessed and says, "*Old Glory, SHE MUST WAVE FOREVER*," and wave forever she shall.

PRIVATE SIDNEY KAPLAN
CHERRY POINT, N.C.
JANUARY 15, 1943

Φ Φ Φ

No More Death

"Who speaks for me?" cries the Israeli child who is the target of death that he neither understands nor controls. *"Who speaks for me?"* asks the pregnant mother who has watched the dead buried the day before and who lives in daily fear of the fate that awaits her unborn child who is the target of rockets that the child may never see nor understand the source.

There is an Arab proverb of deep meaning which says, *"I cried because I had no shoes and then I saw a man who had no feet."*

How do you explain to those who are about to die that life values are unequal? The voices speak out in dismay, politely and lightly, when the color of the victim is not the same as that of the crier of the victims' chosen path to God is different than that of the crier. I abhor the killing of any man, woman or child by other men. What justification can there be in causing the violent death of innocent people?

But how do I explain to my children the fact that though the months that have passed the merciless shelling and killing in pure civilian areas in which there was no military headquarters or major military targets met only the response of indignation of the mighty, or an occasional editorial or cocktail party comment? How do I explain that conduct, not over a period of days, weeks or months or years but generations?

How do I explain a response of horror and the threats or retribution that come to light when the Israeli gunner reciprocates in kind? Reciprocates, not for the purpose of attacking the innocent but for the purpose of destroying the head of the guilty?

May God give strength to the Sadats of this world who sought peace and gave peace. May God give my leaders the wisdom to weigh the decision that they would make if an outlaw guerrilla band rained death and destruction across any of the borders of this land against my fellow countrymen who live in the small country towns, in the villages, in the suburbs or in the hearts of the city far removed from the military might of this land. How long would they allow the rockets to fall?

Mr. Begin may not be 100 percent right with the decisions that he is making, but which of our spokesmen stands 100 percent right with the decisions that they are making?

Sidney Kaplan
Baltimore
8/10/81

Φ Φ Φ

*An answer to ex-V.P. Agnew who blamed his fate
on the fact that the system was corrupt.*

Agnew and Corruption

Are there others who feel the same sickening nausea that comes over me when I view in <u>The Sun</u> a picture of Agnew and read the words attributed to him as stated in the printed article?

The audacity to argue that *"the system is corrupt."* Men make a system. Men create corruption. Neither an Agnew nor any other man can justify his corruption by saying *"the system is corrupt.."*

The only acceptable comment in the September 14 news article is the statement of this man that major contributors rely on favors as a condition for contributions. He is certainly a voice of authority in this field and I readily accept his authoritative comment.

Reviewing the article further, the statement that he makes as to what happened forcing him to resign - *"something happened - something very shocking and shaking to me happened."* Could it be that this something which was both shocking and shaking was the fact that he was caught?

Finally, he comments that Israel is *"a government based on a Talmudic concept."* He states this as though it were a fault. And this is perhaps because Agnew has no conception of what the Talmud truly means.

A government based on the Talmudic concept would be a government based on the very simply stated Ten Commandments. It is a government where the value of life is more meaningful that the value of property.

It is a government where seeds are sown for the establishment of such documentation as the Constitution of the United States of America.

There is no more perfection to the man who is a citizen of Israel than there is to the man who is a citizen of any other country of the world. Perfection in men is truly the proper proportion of imperfections.

It is degrading to have anyone who best deals with others while in a key governmental position behind closed doors for fear of the sunlight to comment on the morals or manners of any person.

Corruption reigns in many facets of our life. No system creates corruption - it is the man who creates the corruption and it is a man who should answer for the corruption he creates no matter what position he occupies.

One cannot be just "*a little bit pregnant*" nor can one be just "*a little bit corrupt.*" Perhaps above all else the values of the young generation are the best guide to refine and to instill in the hearts of men true Talmudic concepts.

Sidney Kaplan
Baltimore

Φ Φ Φ

*To a young client who strayed from the straight and narrow
and who was helped by family and two dear family friends*

"...(on your) behalf by these two men. I hope that should I
ever need the hand of friendship, that such willing sets of
hands are in like manner extended to me.

What is done, is done, and no man can undo. The tragedy of
what has passed can only magnify itself if it has not served
to cause you to take an honest inventory of yourself---Your
wonderful God given abilities, your good health, the treasure
you have found in the way of a wife and family, and the
many friends who have in some small part made themselves
known to you--and to further make you realize that the
destiny of your life and the lives of those dearest to you <u>rest
entirely in in (your) hands</u>...

I am confident that you have a future which will succeed in
direct proportion to your willingness to discover the patience
necessary for success and your willingness to realize that the
best road in life offers no short cuts to the men who walk it."

Φ Φ Φ

To a friend who was discharged
from a 15 year job by a new manager

Life has many cycles, as you so well know. As we start a new cycle, it is more normal than not that we have a tendency to believe that the cycle will never end. Cycles do end.

Φ Φ Φ

In a letter leaving the position
of president of my Congregation

And so it is that this extraordinary life experience must come to an end, as all life experiences must inevitably come to an end.

Φ Φ Φ

To Supreme Justice Anthony M. Kennedy
on His Appointment to the Court

Let Solomon's wisdom
　　Walk with you,
Let your decisions be strong
　　And true;
Let God guide your heart
　　Provide you light
Our destiny rests with
　　Your insight!

Φ Φ Φ

To Supreme Court Justice David H. Suter
on His Appointment to the Court

Law learning and logic
　　Must play their part,
But the judgment of man
　　Comes from the heart.

"God Go With You!"

Φ Φ Φ